Conversations with
My Inner Atheist

⚓

A Christian Apologist Explores
Questions that Keep People Up at Night

2 Cup Press

Canada

2 CUP
PRESS

Conversations with My Inner Atheist

All Scripture quotations, unlss otherwise indicated, are taken from The Holy Bible: *New International Version®, NIV®.* Copyright © 1973, 1978, 1984, 2011 by Biblica, Inc.™ Used by permission of Zondervan. All rights reserved.

ISBN: 978-1-7750462-2-6
ISBN: 978-1-7750462-3-3

Book cover design by Darryl Frayne - steadydigital.ca

For Mom, who likes my books,
but who didn't like this book title.
Don't worry, Mom, I'm still a Christian!

Questions from My Inner Atheist

"I would rather have questions that can't be answered than answers that can't be questioned."

- Richard Feynman-

Secure the Ballast & Raise the Sail

⚓

An Introduction

I grew up in a Pentecostal church that was dominated by a focus on victorious Christian living. We reminded ourselves of the fact every time we would greet each other with this question, "Do you have the victory, brother?" "Sister, are you victorious today?" The answer, of course, was always a hearty "*Amen!*"

An implication of always having the victory was that you've basically got your Christian faith sorted out. Granted, you may still have some unanswered questions—after all, there should always be *a bit of room* for mystery—but you don't have any nagging doubts, any questions that keep you up at night. No, you don't have to worry about that because you have . . . the victory!

I soon discovered that this focus on faith and conviction and the minimization of doubt and questioning that came with it, was not just a trait of the Pentecostals: it was a hallmark of conservative Christianity more generally. Evangelicals and fundamentalists alike would regularly share their confidence in the great things of God. And if they had any doubts at all, you can bet they were quiet about them.

My own shifting relationship with certainty and doubt, confidence and questioning, is reflected in my history with apologetics. Growing up, my search for certainty prompted me to seek answers. As a result, by the time I was in high school I was an avid reader of apologetics. Back in the 1980s there wasn't nearly as much on offer as there is today, but I read my Josh McDowell and John Warwick Montgomery and C.S. Lewis. The goal was to beat back the mystery and get it all figured out. In short, having the *victory* in this area of my life meant having *all the answers*.

This journey continued on through my university years culminating one May afternoon in 1996 just after I started my first seminary class. The class was on the historical Jesus and was being taught by the Australian scholar Paul Barnett. As I was walking back to my car with a fellow student after class, I explained to him why I was taking the course: "I have a good grasp on the other main areas of apologetics," I boasted. "I just need to fill out my understanding of the historical Jesus."

Yes, I actually said that. Apparently, I thought I had it *all* figured out. I just had this one last gap to fill in before I had completed my *vast* education.

Looking back, that moment was a turning point. Even as I heard those words come out of my mouth I winced just a bit. It was like the blinders fell from my eyes as I was forced to confront just how hubristic and naïve I sounded. Gradually, I came to realize that all those years I had focused on getting quick and comprehensive answers, but I had never dared to spend serious time in the stormy seas of genuine doubts and disturbing questions. The result was that I had been left with a grossly distorted perception of my own achievements and an ego that sorely needed to be cut down to size.

I've met many Christians with a similar backstory. They grew up in a church that valorized certainty and rejected doubt. But when they come to that critical moment of questioning and doubting that history, their response is often to toss out certainty altogether. While I understand where they are coming from, I have come to see it a bit differently. I don't think certainty is a problem in itself.

Instead, I believe that certainty can journey with doubt, confidence can welcome questioning, and together they can work to create a healthy and balanced Christian community.

In that respect, I like to compare the critical balance of a healthy Christian community with the metaphor of the ballast and the sails of a sailboat. The ballast keeps the vessel steady, but the sails capture the wind that drives it forward. The effective sailboat needs both the ballast and the sails.

So it is with the Christian community. That community is most balanced when we have both the steadying ballast of calming certainty and settled confidence as well as the billowing sails that channel the power of nagging doubts and incisive questioning. So while there were many problems with the over-emphasis on certainty I had growing up, I am still grateful for the steadying ballast of conviction and certainty that I received in my upbringing. In the words of Paul, "we are more than conquerors through him who loved us" (Romans 8:37) and there is something to be said for living in that victory. That kind of calming confidence is a gift and I first discovered it in my own Pentecostal tradition.

But few people are always living in victory, and there's nothing wrong with those who are not. As the metaphor would suggest, a ship that is all ballast and no sail does not go anywhere. And a Christian community that is all certainty and confidence and no doubt or questioning is likewise in danger of getting caught in the doldrums. So I'm also appreciative of the doubt and questions that I have since come to embrace.

Still, the journey into questioning and doubt is not without risk. Raising the sail can be scary because you simply don't always know where the wind will take you. I'm reminded of an old saying among trial lawyers: while in cross-examination, you never ask a question to which you do not know the answer. It makes sense: a good trial lawyer controls the process and prevents the conversation from going in directions she did not anticipate. For years, that was my view of apologetics: I would never explore a question or topic unless I was sure that I could get all the satisfactory answers I needed. I was one of those people who assumed that you shouldn't raise a problem unless you already know the solution.

But sometimes, just being honest about the problem is the first step *toward* a solution. And raising the sail is living into the fact that you may ask questions for which you do not know the answers. Indeed, you may very well ask a question without knowing whether you will *ever* find a satisfactory answer.

The truth is, *I'd rather accept that there are some questions I may never answer rather than return to the simple days where I thought my answers were beyond question.* The revolution comes in recognizing that *that is okay.* That's what it means to raise the sail and catch the wind. It means giving up control and being willing to live into the questions as they appear on the horizon.

So how does one go about raising their sail? In this book, I look at one simple way to go about it. It is a manner of listening to that voice within, the one that presses doubts and poses questions and often remains dissatisfied with the answers. It's the voice that I learned to silence years ago when I was all about certainty and confidence and ever more answers packed like ballast into the bottom of my boat.

Over the last twenty plus years, I have gradually learned how to listen to that voice more closely and to consider seriously the doubts it presses and the questions it poses. And I've learned that sometimes when that voice is dissatisfied with the answers, maybe I should be as well. In this book, I invite that voice into a no-holds-barred conversation. I have come to call that voice My Inner Atheist—Mia, for short—and throughout this exchange Mia will be giving voice to the skeptic, the doubter, the agnostic, and the atheist.

In the pages that follow, I invite Mia to raise whatever topic she likes. In some cases, Mia acts as a sort of devil's advocate, pushing me to consider the objections and perspectives of my opponents, to see things as they do, to feel the existential draw of their perspective, to try walking a mile in their shoes. In these moments, Mia is exemplifying a practice that philosophers call steelmanning.

Perhaps you've heard of strawmanning, the fallacy of taking an opponent's view and presenting it in a weak form and then rejecting that weak form as if it were the only version on offer. Well, as you can probably guess, steelmanning is the opposite: it consists of taking the views of one's opponent and presenting them in the strongest light possible.

One of the best compliments I can get is when an interlocutor tells me that I stated their position better than they could. That is the goal of steelmanning, but as you can guess, it also brings a risk. For one thing, if you believe the view you are steelmanning is ultimately false, you risk helping your opponent retrench into a position that you believe to be in error. And in that sense, at least, you may not be doing them any favors.

Equally disturbing is the possibility that you might find yourself being persuaded by your own sympathetic defense. In fact, you might even change your own views by steelmanning the views of others. This is a great reminder of the fact that raising your sail also entails giving up control. Asking questions you may not be able to answer and steelmanning your opponent, those are not risk free actions. But frankly, for anyone genuinely concerned about the pursuit of truth, I think these are risks well worth taking.

In other cases, Mia acts as a window into my own ongoing questions and existential doubts. As you can imagine, this is where the greatest vulnerability lies. Do we dare to open up the Pandora's box of our own questions, many of which as yet remain unresolved? At times like this, you may raise the sail expecting a gentle breeze and instead you find that you've unleashed a gale-force wind that threatens to take you in directions you'd rather not go.

Bottom line: there are no guarantees as to how this will unfold. But lest you are inclined to think it is a risk not worth taking, I will say that in my view, the willingness to embark on this risky conversation is actually central to faithful and mature Christian discipleship. God gave his people the name Israel because they are those who wrestle with God (Genesis 32:22-32). As Christians, we're called to a radical life of intellectual honesty, and that includes wrestling with questions and doubt.

Growing up in my Pentecostal church, the last thing we would've considered pious was wrestling with God by asking questions and expressing doubts. We were all about piously packing in the ballast. In the questioning mind we saw only a threat to piety. But it turns out that I could not have been more wrong. When you are free to wrestle with God through questions and doubts, you show the depth of your relationship with God: no conversation is off limits. That act itself is indicative of piety, trust, and intimacy with God. And that is what it means to be true Israel. When we are willing to join in our own wrestling with the inner voice of questioning, we are demonstrating true Israel lived in our own lives.

Okay, that's enough by way of introduction. Mia, the floor is yours and nothing is off limits. Growing up, I was encouraged to silence you. But in this book I'm giving you free rein to consider any question you like.

So take it away. . .

1

⛵

Why should we listen to apologists when they're really just selling a product?

Mia: Seriously? Are you sure you're ready to jump right in?

Randal: Yeah, go ahead. Have at it.

Mia: Fair enough, you asked for it. But this new-found freedom to speak my mind is going to take some getting used to. You spent several years in your youth trying to keep me quiet, out of sight and out of mind.

Randal: Sorry about that. At least, I'm making up for lost time.

Mia: Well okay, better late than never, I guess. Believe me, I've got a lot to say and I'd like to get warmed up by challenging the notion of apologetics itself.

Randal: Oh?

Mia: Yes sir! Here's my first question: Why should we listen to apologists when you're really just selling a product? Think about cars for a moment. You're not like the guy who is working for an independent consumer advocacy agency like JD Power and Associates or Consumer Reports, doing objective surveys of customer satisfaction and developing objective tests to evaluate every car maker.

Instead, you're like the Ford salesman working the lot, committed to selling Fords to would-be customers. So while you claim to be committed to reason and evidence, the fact is that you're *invested*, your intellectual integrity is compromised, you're a *salesman*.

Randal: Not the first time I've heard *that* objection. So, it's important to begin with some basics. First off, apologetics just means to give a defense. It is not something specifically religious or Christian: it can apply to any belief whatever that belief may be.

So to consider a mundane example, some years ago my wife got a Dyson vacuum cleaner to replace our sturdy old Electrolux. At first, I didn't see the point because I thought the Electrolux worked just fine. But then we did a little experiment. First, we vacuumed the living room with our Electrolux and then we vacuumed it again with the Dyson. Rolling over the same carpet with the Dyson we picked up half a canister more of dust and dog fur, all of it missed on the first pass by the Electrolux.

I couldn't believe it! From that day forward, I was sold. And you know what happened after that? I began telling other people about what a great product the Dyson was and how they really should try one for themselves. Without even realizing it, I naturally became an apologist for Dyson. And that was because I thought I had an important belief and I valued other people, so I naturally shared my positive experience with them.

Mia: And just to be clear, you're *not* being paid by Dyson right now, are you?

Randal: Um, no. I wish! But as I was just suggesting, there are two basic factors that must be in place for apologetics. First, you must have a belief that you value as important. And second, you must value other people such that you want them to gain that important belief. If you've got those two factors, you've got apologetics.

So when you say that I'm invested in my beliefs, yeah, sure, in one sense I am. But that's true of all of us. Nobody comes to the conversation neutral. We all come invested with a commitment to what we currently believe and to persuading others of it. And that is fully consistent with intellectual integrity.

To put it another way, if I'm a salesman then we're *all* salespeople.

Mia: Uh, I get that you want to pretend that I'm selling something but I'm really not. I'm just asking questions.

Randal: Yeah, I've heard that before. But the person who declines to take a position and instead only asks questions has also taken a position. The skeptic or questioner is the person who is implicitly saying that the answers provided thus far do not yet warrant belief: that is also a position.

And note that you've already commended the view that one should be like a car tester working for Consumer Reports rather than a salesman working for Ford. So *that's what you're selling*. That's what you're an apologist for. You're also invested; you're just pitching a different message.

Mia: No, I'm not. I'm just saying that you should be objective.

Randal: I agree: we *all* should be objective. That doesn't change the fact that you clearly do have a view and since you're trying to persuade me of yours, you're being an apologist for it. Hey, don't get me wrong: I don't see any problem with that just so long as you recognize that you are invested too.

Mia: Well then, how about I put it this way: not all products are equally good. And I think being an advocate for objective testing of cars is way better than selling them.

Randal: Again, just to be clear, that's the position *you're* selling. Furthermore, the way you describe it is a classic false dichotomy. What if a person has done their due diligence, they've looked at all the cars available, and they honestly think that a particular car maker has the best products? Then they can sell those cars and be an advocate for them—they are indeed invested—but that isn't at the expense of their intellectual integrity. On the contrary, it is a direct expression of their intellectual integrity.

What is more, a salesman can always give honest advice. If another car or brand would suit the customer better, he can always let them know. That's how I'd approach being a salesman.

So again, I think your either/or is a classic false dichotomy. One can have intellectual integrity *and* be an advocate for a particular position. You don't have to choose.

Mia: Oh yeah? You want me to believe that if you think another car is better you'd tell the customer to shop elsewhere? I doubt it.

Randal: Since I'm a Christian, I believe that Christianity is true and offers the fullest and most correct understanding of reality. But that doesn't prevent me from recognizing where there are weaknesses in my beliefs and strengths in the beliefs of others. In fact, doing that expresses an intellectual integrity that ultimately serves an apologist's self-interest. You see, there is really nothing more important to an apologist than credibility. And there's no better way to gain and maintain credibility than through objectivity and honesty.

Mia: It sounds duplicitous to me, as if you're honest about weaknesses and difficulties and questions in your position merely as a sort of gambit, a roundabout strategy to get more 'sales' by the end of the month.

Randal: No, not at all. It's simply a fact that an honest salesman will do better in the long run because people will trust him. That said, you don't seek to be honest just to gain people's trust. You do it because it's the right thing to do: the fact that trust comes in the wake of honesty is a natural consequence of doing the right thing, that's all.

So I'm not suggesting you should be objective and honest merely to get people to be more likely to accept your arguments. Rather, I'm pointing out that while it is simply the right thing to do to be objective and honest, it also has the benefit of increasing the credibility of the apologist and thus the likelihood that folks will seriously consider his or her arguments.

2

How can a Christian academic have intellectual freedom?

Mia: Let me try this from a slightly different angle. I'm willing to concede the general point that people who ask questions have a position and are, to some degree, invested in defending a point-of-view. But you're not out of the woods yet. Your next problem is that you're employed by a Christian seminary.

Randal: Yes indeed, that is true.

Mia: And as an employee of that school, you have to sign off on a statement of faith, right?

Randal: Yes, in this case, the North American Baptist Statement of Beliefs.[1]

---

[1] https://nabconference.org/wp-content/uploads/2019/02/2.-NAB-State-ment-of-Beliefs-and-Affirmation-of-Marriage-ADOPTED-by-Triennial-Delegates-July-5-2012_0-1.pdf

Mia: So as an apologist you have to measure up to that. You have to make sure that you don't violate it. That statement is a constraint on your intellectual freedom and thus your intellectual *integrity*.

Randal: Not so fast! First off, you need to keep in mind that the institutional requirement of adherence to a particular statement is *self-selecting*. If I wasn't on board with the statement, I wouldn't be teaching at the school in the first place. So people will apply to work at a particular Christian school if they are in harmony with the school's statement. And those who don't fit won't apply.

Mia: Fine, but then what happens if you change your mind? Then you can't be honest about it unless you want to face the chopping block. So the requirements of your institution undermine your intellectual integrity, like I said.

Randal: I agree that there are expectations: call them constraints if you like. But again, I'd want to point out that that is true of membership in any belief community or institution. Every institution places some kind of expectations in terms of belief and practice on members or participants.

Mia: Not *all*, like not atheist or freethought groups, for example.

Randal: Are you kidding? Those groups *definitely* have their own expectations. Imagine that Jones gets a job as a speaker and fundraiser for the group American Atheists. If Jones then converted to Christianity, do you think that American Atheists would keep him around?

Mia: I think he wouldn't *want* to hang around.

Randal: That's a deflection. Whether he wanted to hang around or not, he'd be gone. The reason is simple: you can't represent an atheist group if you're a Christian. And that judgment comes

as surely from the atheists as it comes from the Christians. So a
Baptist seminary is not the only institution with expectations. A
group like American Atheists has them as well.

Mia: Okay, *maybe*, but the demands of your group are a lot more
extensive and the vision is a lot narrower.

Randal: More extensive? Maybe, but then how extensive is *too
extensive*? It depends on whom you ask, right?

As for 'narrower', that's clearly a value judgment on your part.
If the framework provided is the correct one, it isn't narrow, by
definition. And no surprise, I believe the framework to which I'm
committed is indeed correct.

The fact is that we're all on a spectrum in regard to our partic-
ipation in various belief communities and institutions. So if you
want to insist that some particular point on that spectrum is just
too far, you owe an explanation as to what point that is and why.

I suspect that in most cases, people are merely saying any community or institution that requires more in terms of belief or
practice than *their* community or institution is 'too much.' But that's
really no better than people who reserve the label 'fundamentalist'
for anybody more conservative than them. It's purely a person
relative judgment and, as such, *it doesn't mean much.*

And as I suggested above when I talked about self-selection,
if a person is a fit for the belief and practice expectations of a
community or institution then the whole question of extensiveness
or narrowness really becomes something of a moot point. If the
person can flourish within that institution because they share the
same beliefs and values then they are free to work within those
self-chosen constraints. Indeed, they aren't *constraints* at all.

Think about it like this: a sports car is not lacking freedom
because it stays on the street instead of going off-road. It is built for
the street and that's where it runs best. And for me, if I'm built for
the Christian/baptist street and various non-Christian alternatives
are the equivalent of dirt roads, then I'm not losing out by staying

on the street where I can achieve my maximum potential instead of going offroad where I'd just spin my tires.

Mia: So in this scenario are you supposed to be like Lightning McQueen or something?

Randal: Hah! You could definitely do worse. And it is also worth keeping in mind that as far as the spectrum goes, Christian institutions are all over the map in terms of belief expectations: some have more expectations and others fewer. So I really don't see the point of singling out particular Christian institutions as lacking intellectual freedom.

Mia: I dunno, man, I looked at your Statement of Belief and it's a pretty long list of stuff to sign off on. Maybe you're right that we're all on the spectrum but it seems to me that you're pretty far out. If there are many streets, the ones available to you are particularly limited and narrow. And at some point the limited number of narrow streets is a real world constraint on your intellectual freedom and integrity.

Randal: This is a good moment to say more about what a confessional statement like this is and how it functions because I think you're getting the wrong impression. When you read the North American Baptist Statement of Beliefs you need to keep in mind that it is not intended to function as a creed where you need to sign onto every jot and tittle of the document or you get turfed. Rather, it functions as a centering document, a set of basic claims around which we gather with some legitimate room for a diversity of interpretation and application.

A statement like the NAB Statement of Beliefs includes many claims and not all of them are of equal import. There is room to interpret many of the claims and those interpretations are often established over time within community. In addition, the Baptist tradition has a strong emphasis upon *soul competency* which appeals to the idea that every individual is responsible to his/her conscience and reason, presumably informed and guided by the Holy Spirit, to read and draw their own conclusions about faith and practice. As a result, there should be a high tolerance for differences of opinion. Indeed, I'd be willing to submit that some degree of difference in opinion enriches a community much as iron sharpens iron.

Mia: But Baptists are kind of famous for splitting off, aren't they? You know the old joke about the Baptist stranded alone on a desert island? When he's finally rescued the rescuers discover three grass huts. And the Baptist explains, "The first hut is my house, the second one is the church I go to, and the third one is the church I used to go to."

Randal: Ba dum tsss! Yeah, I've heard that one before . . . more than once as it turns out. And I get the point of the humor: Baptists, in particular, don't always live up to the ideal vision I'm presenting. But I do think that generally speaking, we should appreciate the expansive and inclusive function of confessional documents in the Protestant—and specifically Baptistic—tradition as well as the role for soul competency in discerning and articulating one's own views.

Mia: Okay, well I have a feeling we're about to see how competent your soul is!

3

⚓

If the Gospel is simple,
why doesn't the Bible simply present it?

Mia: Enough with the niggling introductory stuff about intellectual freedom and the like. Let's jump right in to some big questions. I want to look at the problem of the Gospel. If God wants to save everyone, then presumably he would make the Gospel simple and accessible for everyone, right?

Randal: That's right, and *he did*. There are ocean depths in the Gospel that can occupy the minds of the greatest theologian for a lifetime. But it is also beautifully simple and straightforward such that it can be grasped by the mind of a child.

Mia: Really, eh? Well, if the Gospel is so simple, why doesn't the Bible simply present it?

Randal: What do you mean? It does.

Mia: You think so? Okay, how about you summarize that simple Gospel, you know, the one so simple that it can be grasped by any child.

Randal: Glad to. "For God so loved the world that he gave his . . ."

Mia: "Only Son," yeah I get it. Yadda yadda yadda: you're just going to cite John 3:16? That's it?

Randal: Is there something wrong with that?

Mia: Yeah, at least two things, actually. First, why did you go to that verse, specifically?

Randal: What do you mean?

Mia: What I mean is, your answer highlights a verse beloved of evangelical Protestants, one that *they* commonly use to summarize the Gospel. But nowhere does the Bible itself say that this specific verse is the key to unlock the whole. You bring that assumption to the text. And that means it isn't that simple. You need to start with the instruction from somebody else directing you to look to *that* verse as the key.

Randal: I'm not sure I see the basis of your complaint. Sure, we *all* come to the Bible from a way of reading. But our traditions can simply help us clarify that simple Gospel. Anyway, what was your second thing?

Mia: Right, the second thing is that I want *details*. Be specific. Don't just give me a proof-text. Tell me specifically *how a particular individual is actually saved.*

Randal: Wait, you asked for a simple statement. *Now* you want details? Make up your mind.

Mia: Come on, I think you can figure out what I'm asking. John 3:16 gives a general description, but what I'm asking is specifically how each individual is supposed to be saved. Think about it like this: if a volcano is about to cover Paradise Island in lava, it isn't enough to tell me that the government sent a boat to evacuate the island. I need to know when and where to go to get on the boat.

That's the kind of thing I'm asking for now: *specific details.* For example, do you need to pray a sinner's prayer? If so, what does it need to include? Does it need to use Jesus' name or mention that he's divine? Repentance for sins? And when do you need to pray it? You know, stuff like that.

Randal: Okay, I see what you mean. The good news is that Paul actually offers that kind of detail in Romans 10:9: "If you declare with your mouth, 'Jesus is Lord,' and believe in your heart that God raised him from the dead, you will be saved."

Mia: Great, so that's it? Believe those two propositions and you're saved?

Randal: That's what Paul says.

Mia: Huh, that's strange, because when Jesus talks about salvation in Matthew 25:31-46 as that which separates the sheep from the goats, he doesn't appeal to those two propositions at all. Rather, he appeals to *works.* The sheep are those who *do certain things,* not those who *believe two propositions.* So maybe it isn't quite as simple as you suggested?

Randal: Well, it might help if we can view our answers as contextualized. For example, one area where Christians sometimes struggle is with the area of assurance: how can I know that I'm saved? I wouldn't respond to every query about assurance the same way, however. Instead, I'd respond in a way that is fine-tuned to each individual asking the question.

If Smith really struggles with knowing that God loves her I would remind her that nothing can separate her from the love of God (Romans 8:28) or I might refer to Jesus' promise that he will lose none of those the Father has given him (John 6:39).

But if Smith is living it up and not taking her faith seriously I might be inclined to speak instead of Jesus' sobering warning you just mentioned about the sheep and goats. What I'd say would be shaped by the person and the context. In short, it depends what people need to hear in the moment.

Mia: Okay, but note how you're now making it even *more* complicated. I think we need to return to the illustration I gave of needing to evacuate Paradise Island in order to escape the impending volcanic explosion. It isn't enough to say that there's a boat being sent to evacuate. You also need to tell me where to go to get to that boat. If Romans 10:9 is telling me to go to the dock on the east side of the island, Matthew 25:31-46 might as well be telling me to go to the beach on the *opposite* side of the island.

And that just makes no sense. No government that wanted to safely evacuate everyone would give ambiguous, conflicting instructions. People are in imminent danger of getting buried in boiling mud and lava. They need clear instructions. So why doesn't God give those clear instructions?

Randal: Well, the thing to keep in mind is that we don't come to this question as individuals. The church has creeds that provide a framework for understanding. The Apostles' Creed, for example, centers us on the main thing. It may not answer every question but it gets the big picture.

Mia: Once again, I need to point out that your response is to make matters even more complicated. You're like the guy struggling in quicksand who sinks deeper in every time he flails his arms. I'm pointing out the lack of clarity in the Bible on the precise details that are required to be saved. And your response is to appeal to a tradition. That's just making it worse as there is no shortage of Christian traditions!

Imagine if we were in a hotel and I pointed out that the emergency map for escaping the building that was posted on the door was hopelessly vague. It wouldn't help matters if you then noted that the bedside drawer included two incompatible interpretation keys. Which key is the right one? And why include answer keys in the first place let alone two conflicting ones? *Why not just post all the necessary information on the door map itself?*

By the same token, which tradition are we supposed to appeal to in order to get it right? You've cited a creed, but Christians disagree on which creeds provide the necessary key and other Christians disagree on whether you should even use creedal 'keys' in the first place.

As a case in point, you cited the Apostles' Creed but that creed isn't used in Eastern Orthodoxy which is another massive and ancient church tradition. And you also conceded that the Apostles' Creed doesn't even provide the kind of detail I'm looking for, the kind of detail we should *all* look for. If I need to evacuate the island, I need precise details about where to go. Don't just tell me a boat is coming. I need to know *how to get on it.* So by invoking tradition you've only made the matter worse: you've added another layer of complexity. And with that, the very idea of a simple Gospel recedes further into the distance.

Randal: Okay, you clearly like your Paradise Island illustration so let's stick with it. You've been assuming that if the government provides somewhat ambiguous instructions that will lead to people who wanted to evacuate quite literally *missing the boat.*

But what if that just isn't the case? What if the government knows exactly what it is doing and the instructions it provides are precisely the best way to get the maximum number of people safely off the island? And what if the apparent ambiguity of the instructions in fact makes perfect sense from the perspective of the government's evacuation strategy?

Mia: *What if?* We can spin endless 'what ifs'. But the question is whether that is what you would *expect*.

Randal: I agree that if the sole purpose of the Bible is to serve as emergency instructions to evacuate planet earth with maximum clarity and efficiency then it fails in its purpose. But I think that's an excellent reason to reject the assumption that that is the Bible's purpose. And given that I believe God surely desires to save the maximum number of people possible, then the Bible does not fail in achieving the end for which God *has* purposed it.

Mia: And what is this mysterious purpose?

Randal: Paul lays it out in 2 Timothy 3:14-17:

> [14] But as for you, continue in what you have learned and have become convinced of, because you know those from whom you learned it, [15] and how from infancy you have known the Holy Scriptures, which are able to make you wise for salvation through faith in Christ Jesus. [16] All Scripture is God-breathed and is useful for teaching, rebuking, correcting and training in righteousness, [17] so that the servant of God may be thoroughly equipped for every good work.

Here Paul says the Scriptures are to make us wise to salvation and then he explains what that means. It means that they are God-breathed—that is, inspired—such that they teach, rebuke, correct, and train us to make us more like Jesus, equipping us for good works.

Paul's whole focus is not about a quick evacuation. Rather, it is to transform people into becoming little Christs who can be his hands and feet in the world and prepare the way for his return. That's the real purpose of the Bible.

Mia: I mean, that's great and all but I must note that by this point the simple Gospel message I was searching for has disappeared over the horizon. Why should we trust that people won't miss the boat because of these very confusing directions?

Randal: I think the problem lies with your illustration. You assume that there is just one way down to one specific dock and if people don't receive very specific instructions then they've missed the boat and are fated to die on the island.

But there is no reason to hold that assumption. There could be many ways to the boat and the instructions that are provided which, while lacking the specificity we might like, may be perfectly capable of achieving that end.

I have no doubt, as I said, that God will be maximally effective at drawing the maximum number of people to himself. There is not just one path to God's boat—as if everyone must pray a specific prayer with just that cognitive content that Paul summarizes in Romans 10:9.

And again, your whole picture is based on the premise of a frantic evacuation. But as that passage in 2 Timothy suggests, that image misconstrues the role of Scripture in salvation. It isn't just an act of getting off an island of death. It's a matter of being formed into the image of God in Jesus Christ. We are called to become like him. And I think it is perfectly reasonable to expect that one significant aspect of the ambiguities and lack of clarity in some of the details of salvation pertains to God's purpose in forming us into particular kinds of persons. If God is who Christians believe him to be then this lack of clarity is not a bug, it's a *feature* because it follows that Scripture is far more effective at achieving God's ends than your minimalistic evacuation map ever could be.

The Bible is a complex library of texts written in three ancient languages—Hebrew, Aramaic, and Greek—and in cultural contexts foreign to the contemporary reader. They show theological diversity and development. They are written in a multiplicity of genres and make copious literary and historical references unfamiliar to the reader today. But presumably that's what God wanted. He didn't want a simple map. He wanted to give us this delightfully complex book.

And I, for one, am grateful.

Mia: You may be grateful, but *I* still don't have an answer to the question I asked.

4

⛵

How can the God of the Philosophers be the God of Abraham, Isaac, and Jacob?

Mia: I have a feeling you just danced around that last question but fine, whatever: here's another problem. And this one goes to the heart of what Christians say about God.

Randal: Sounds good, I'm ready.

Mia: Okay, here goes. The God of the Bible is a being who has emotions (John 3:16; Psalm 5:5), he grows angry (Psalm 106:40), learns (Genesis 18:21), changes his mind (Jonah 3:10), has regrets (Genesis 6:6), has a body and face (Exodus 33:18-20), and sits on a throne (Psalm 103:19). That's how the Bible describes God.

But then theologians and philosophers come along and say, oh, no, wait, God doesn't *actually* have emotions, he doesn't *really* grow angry. He doesn't learn or change his mind; in fact, he has no regrets, no body, face or throne on which he sits. Instead, here's what God *really* is: he is an impassible, eternal, non-physical, omnipresent, omniscient, and omnipotent being. Yeah, that's it!

In other words, he's completely different from the being actually described in the Bible.

Forgive me, but it looks like you're trying to fit a square peg in a round hole. When you have two completely different descriptions the only conclusion is that these aren't the same being at all. How can the God of the Bible be the same being as this God of the Philosophers? You need to choose!

Randal: Yes, many people have sensed that tension. Your framing is well chosen, too: the great French philosopher Pascal famously attributed a mystical experience he had to "the God of Abraham, Isaac, and Jacob, not the God of the Philosophers."

Mia: Great minds think alike.

I'll level with you here: it seems to me that the reason theologians and philosophers gravitate to the God of the Philosophers is because they are *embarrassed* by the God of the Bible. They don't know what to do with him. He isn't sophisticated and respectable. He appears capricious, mean, and unpredictable. He's a finite being, located in spacetime and he has a body and learns and has regrets: in other words, he is little more than a glorified human being, no different in that respect than the gods of ancient Greece.

Randal: I understand that that may be your perception, but maybe I can help you with your incredulity. Imagine, for a moment the response of an average man when he first learns that according to the scientists, the heavy oak chair on which he is sitting is composed of vibrating packets of energy in empty space. Picture *his* incredulity. No doubt, he'd be thinking *how can you possibly hope to unify these two utterly incompatible pictures of reality?* A heavy oak chair that is somehow also vibrating packets of energy in empty space? It makes no sense. Obviously these are really just two different things, right?

But of course, it *does* make sense if one can understand that these are both legitimate descriptions and that they operate at different explanatory levels. The description of a heavy oak chair captures the everyday experience while the description of vibrating packets of energy provides the physicist's description of that same reality.

By analogy, the God who acts in history, who learns, changes his mind, grows angry and the like may capture the perception of the everyday Christian. At the same time, the theologian describes God as having particular attributes such as eternality, impassibility, and omnipresence.

Mia: I have no problem with the basic idea of how a physicist arrives at her description of the oak chair. But how do you justify moving from the God of Abraham, Isaac, and Jacob to that abstraction debated by theologians and philosophers?

Randal: The first thing you need to recognize is that theology is not simply a product of reading the Bible and counting up the verses that support your view. Rather, it is a matter of reading the Bible in a complex process of reflective equilibrium.

Mia: Reflective *what?*

Randal: You reflect on Scripture in light of your rational and moral intuitions and reasoning, the reading traditions of your background community—like the priority of John 3:16 in understanding salvation—and personal and communal experience. All of these sources inform theological reasoning and together we can see how they bring a theologian stepwise from the experience of the person in the pew to the technical description of God employed by the professional theologian or philosopher.

Mia: That all sounds nice, but unless you can fill in the details, I'm going to suspect you are merely trying to justify the fact that you want to ignore all the Bible's embarrassing details.

Randal: Pardon me, but can *you* fill in all the details from the quantum description of the chair to the experience of the man sitting in it?

Mia: Who's askin'?

Randal: Yeah, I didn't think so. So maybe you could cut me some slack.

Mia: I don't claim to be a physicist. But, uh, you *do* claim to be a theologian.

Randal: Touché. Okay, perhaps I can say a bit more about one specific topic of theology: metaphysics.

Mia: 'Metaphysics' as in crystals and gurus and auras?

Randal: Goodness no, I mean metaphysics as in the area of philosophy that concerns our basic convictions about the structure and nature of the world. Just as everyone engages in philosophical reflection so everyone has a metaphysic, a set of beliefs about the nature of ultimate reality.

A very basic part of philosophical reflection involves turning our drive for conceptual clarification toward our basic metaphysical commitments. As I said, the fact is that everyone has a philosophy and a metaphysic whether we recognize it or not, and it is important to become aware of what our philosophical views are and how they shape our thinking. As Fergus Kerr observes,

> If theologians proceed in the belief that they need neither examine nor acknowledge their inherited metaphysical commitments, they will simply remain prisoners of whatever philosophical school was in the ascendant 30 years earlier, when they were first year students.[2]

---

[2] *Theology After Wittgenstein* (Oxford: Blackwell, 1986), 3.

So it's not like I'm reading the Bible through my philosophy and metaphysic while the guy who believes God literally experiences emotion and changes his mind is free of philosophy and metaphysics. Rather, we're both interpreting the text and engaging in theological and philosophical reflection as we go. As Alister McGrath puts it, philosophical theology is simply concerned with "the clarification of ideas."[3] And we could all use more clarity in our thinking about God. So the question is not whether we shall think theologically and philosophically about these issues but rather whether we will do it *well*.

Mia: But I'm still not clear how you actually get to that philosopher's abstraction based on the earthy and very human depiction of God in the Bible.

Randal: It might help to consider how we get to one big metaphysical claim in particular—the claim that God is *perfect*—*because a lot flows from that one claim*. The great medieval philosopher Anselm argued that when you reflect on the concept of God you arrive at a definition like this: God is that being than which none greater can be conceived.

Mia: Huh? What's that even supposed to mean?

Randal: Put simply, it means that God is the greatest possible being, there is none greater. Now I have surveyed seminary students for almost twenty years by asking them "Do you think God is the most perfect being there could be?" Time and again, they agree. In all that time, I've never had a single student say that God would be anything less than perfect. They might question our grasp of perfection, but they don't question that God *is* perfect.

   I think their intuitions in that regard are spot on. And that means that if we encounter passages in the Bible that depict God acting

---

[3] *Christian Theology: An Introduction*, 6th ed. (Wiley Blackwell, 2017), 91.

in ways that appear to be very far from perfect, we have one of two options: we can either revise our understanding of perfection or we can revise our reading of the passage in question.

So for example, the Bible depicts God changing his mind, having regrets, learning, growing angry, hating people, lashing out in rage, and so on.

Are these behaviors consistent with perfection? Christian theologians will disagree. But what I would hope we can appreciate is that when a theologian ends up with an understanding of God that looks rather different from some of the depictions in the Bible, she did not arrive at that picture by plucking it arbitrarily out of thin air. Rather, she reasoned to it carefully, informed by several factors including a basic intuitive conception of perfection read in critical dialogue with Scripture and informed by tradition, personal experience, and reason.

Thus, we can conclude that the one God that exists necessarily is the God of Abraham, Isaac, and Jacob. Just as the heavy oak chair is the same object as that particular collection of vibrating packets of energy so the God of Abraham, Isaac, and Jacob is the same perfect being as is described by the philosophers. The next step in each case is to explore various models to justify these identity claims and reconcile any tension between them. And that's what systematic theology is all about.

Admittedly, that was a very quick summary, but hopefully you can at least get a sense of how one can unite these two seemingly incompatible conceptions of God.

5

⛵

How do you make sense of the Trinity?

Mia: I'd love to see how *you* actually explain the claim that the God of Abraham, Isaac, and Jacob is perfect, but I also know we need to keep going. Anyway, the problems with God may start there but they definitely don't end there. So let's consider another big question: how do you make sense of the Trinity?

Christians often say that the Trinity is an absolutely essential, foundational doctrine. I've heard Christian theologians say that the Trinity changes how we think about nearly everything. And yet, so far as I can see, the doctrine itself is very confused. That confusion begins with the way people talk about God. One can rightly wonder how it makes sense to say a doctrine which generates such confusion is essential for Christian belief, let alone that it is so key to understanding everything else. Seems to me that's like saying the only way to see the world is by looking through a nearly opaque pair of glasses.

Randal: Ouch! That seems a bit harsh. Maybe you'd like to give an example of this confusion of which you speak?

Mia: I'd love to. It's easy enough to give an example of an average Christian talking about the Trinity with confusion but that's low hanging fruit. So let me give you an example from a learned theologian. This is a quote from a devotional by the theologian Cornelius Plantinga Jr. He writes: "What is God like? God is fatherly and motherly, as Isaiah 42:14 and other passages tell us. God is great and holy. God is like Jesus Christ, his Son. God is, finally and everlastingly, triune."[4]

Randal: Sounds okay to me. So what's the problem?

Mia: What's the problem? It's confused! Plantinga starts out by distinguishing God from Jesus whom he calls God's 'Son'. And then, without missing a beat, he says God is triune. But hold on, a second ago Plantinga was presumably talking about God the Father because that's the agent who is the Father of Jesus. But now, without missing a beat, he describes this same God—the Father—as the Trinity.

Like I said, confused.

Randal: I see what you're saying. Yeah, that might seem confused but at this point I remember the famous words of the fourth century theologian Gregory Nazianzen: "No sooner do I conceive of the One than I am illumined by the splendour of the Three; no sooner do I distinguish Them than I am carried back to the One."[5] Perhaps that is the way to think about it. Maybe that which you interpret as confusion is, from Plantinga's perspective, merely the lived out dynamic tension of the triune God as we move seamlessly between the one and the three.

Mia: "Lived out dynamic tension"? Honestly, if I had a dollar for every time I've heard a Christian appeal to that Gregory quote as

---

4 *Beyond Doubt: Faith-Building Devotions on Questions Christians Ask* (Eerdmans, 2001), 24.
5 Cited in Colin Gunton, *The One, the Three and the Many: God, Creation and the Culture of Modernity* (Cambridge University Press, 1993), 149.

a way to cover up or excuse basic confusion, I'd be rich. Plantinga is not exploring dynamic tension between God as one and God as three. Rather, he's simply *conflating* God the Father with God the Trinity. God the Father is not identical to God the Trinity. And that's pretty obvious because for any two things A and B, if A has one property lacked by B, then A cannot be identical to (i.e. the same thing as) B. So, for example, if God is the Father, and the Father is not three persons then God cannot be three persons.

Randal: Come on, Plantinga is using God in *two* senses: God as God the Father, the first person *of* the Trinity, and God *as* the Trinity of which the Father is the first person. There need be no contradiction. How about a little bit of charity?

Mia: I see, so then you agree that Plantinga is confused because he *conflated* those two distinct conceptions, God as Father and God as Trinity. By your own admission, these are *not* the same thing. And it doesn't matter how many times you quote Gregory Naziansus to cover it up: it's still confused.

Randal: Well, maybe he did get a bit tripped up in his language.

Mia: A bit? There is nothing more basic when it comes to relationship with God than one's ability to *refer* to him . . . or 'them'. And yet, Christians clearly don't know how to refer to the one 'triune' God. All you need for evidence of that is to look at the fact that Plantinga's wording refers to the one triune God with a singular personal pronoun.

Randal: In fairness, you got to admit that it would be very strange to say "Y'all" when praying to the one God.

Mia: Strange, perhaps. But at least it would be consistent. Here, you might be interested in this argument that I came up with which aims to highlight the problem with the way that Christians refer to God:

1. If it is proper to refer to an entity with a singular personal pronoun then that entity is a distinct person.
2. It is proper to refer to the Father, Son, and Spirit each with a singular personal pronoun.
3. Therefore, the Father, Son, and Spirit each is a distinct person.
4. It is proper to refer to the Trinity with a singular personal pronoun.
5. Therefore, the Trinity is a distinct person.
6. The Trinity is not identical to any one of these persons: Father, Son, or Spirit.
7. Therefore, the Trinity is a distinct person from the Father, Son, and Spirit.
8. Therefore, Christians believe God is four persons: Trinity, Father, Son, and Spirit.
9. The doctrine of the Trinity says that God is three persons.
10. Therefore, Christians should reject the doctrine of the Trinity.

Randal: Wow, that's a mouthful. I see you have been thinking about this. Okay, well if I may wade into the debate, I think it would make sense for the Christian to reject the first premise of your argument. I don't think it follows that use of a singular personal pronoun always warrants the conclusion that the referent of the pronoun is a single person.

It is important to keep in mind that we're dealing here not with logic so much as the conventional limitations of a specific language, in this case, English. And English does not rigorously bind the singularity/plurality of pronouns to the singularity or plurality of the referent(s) of those pronouns.

For example, in English, we have a convention of using a plural pronoun to refer to an individual. It is known as the so-called *royal we* as when a single king declares: "We hereby decree . . ."

English also has a less familiar (but still correct) practice of using the plural 'we' to refer to an individual such as when a wife says to her husband "We need to mow the lawn" even as she *actually* means to say "*you* need to mow the lawn".

Mia: Fine, but where are the cases where a singular pronoun refers to more than one person?

Randal: Well, given these other *deviations* from standard usage, it would certainly be possible. But what is more, one could argue that we already have examples of what you're looking for precisely in the standard Christian usage of a singular personal pronoun to refer to God. In that case, if we can become self-conscious that we are following a linguistic convention when doing this, rather than positing a fourth person of the Trinity, we could recognize that this convention is actually quite well established, at least in Christian language. Suffice it to say, we have excellent grounds to conclude that premise (1) fails and your argument goes with it.

Mia: You may think you've neutralized the argument with your pained and idiosyncratic use of pronouns, but at the very least my excellent argument highlights widespread confusion among Christians.

And that brings me back to the heart of my concern. Christian theologians claim that the doctrine of the Trinity is a required pillar of orthodox confession, one that illumines all other matters of doctrine. But the doctrine itself is very hard to understand and confusion about it is rife. And that is not only the case among average people but also among academic theologians as my Plantinga example shows.

Randal: I admit that confusion is a problem. And I also agree that the statements which are commonly made by contemporary theologians about how the Trinity illumines all manner of other doctrine are often overstated. But perhaps you could consider it an overcorrection for the fact that the doctrine was neglected for a long period of the church.

As for the paradox at the heart of the Trinity, I think we should have grace for the theology of our neighbors. Solving the mystery of the Trinity is not a prerequisite for making it into God's

Kingdom. The Christian believes there is one God and that God is three distinct and equally divine persons: Father, Son, and Spirit. Many theologians have proposed intriguing analogies and theories to explain the logic of this relationship that are faithful to Scripture, tradition, and popular piety, and I'm okay with that.

Mia: Whoa, I didn't think you'd be playing the mystery card this soon!

Randal: Keep in mind that Christians aren't the only ones who appeal to mystery. For example, atheist philosopher Colin McGinn has written a lot on mystery from the perspective of an atheist. To note one example, he has argued that the mind/brain problem—that is, how the material brain produces and relates to the conscious mind—may be impossible for us to solve.[6] He calls his position *mysterianism*, and it's a fascinating idea. If McGinn is okay with playing the 'mystery card' regarding how the mind works, I think I'm okay playing it with respect to the fundamental nature of the triune God.

Mia: Just as long as you don't play it *too* often. It's not a get out of jail free card, you know.

---

[6] See Colin McGinn, *The Mysterious Flame: Conscious Minds in a Material World* (Basic Books, 2000).

6

⛵

If the Bible includes immoral laws, how can it be inspired?

Mia: Okay, let's turn back to the Bible for a moment.

Randal: I had a feeling we weren't done with that topic.

Mia: Done? We're just getting started. So I already pointed out that the Bible is surprisingly ambiguous in laying out the details of salvation. The problem I now want to consider is that the authors of Scripture say a lot of other things which are morally problematic and thus they count against the Bible being the revelation of any perfect God of the Philosophers. Maybe the God of Abraham, Isaac, and Jacob is behind this book. But if he is, he ends up looking more like a terrifying Middle Eastern warlord rather than the vision of Anselm's perfect idealization.

Randal: Hey, easy on the Richard Dawkins-styled rhetoric.

Mia: *Rhetoric?* Have you *read* the Bible? It's full of immoral teaching.

Randal: I'll stop you right there. Be careful about conflating that which is *recorded* in the Bible with that which is *taught* in the Bible. The Bible includes lots of material that is simply recorded but not commended.

Mia: Fine, let me clarify. The Bible includes many passages in which the human authors—God's people—endorse behaviors or actions that are evil. And these are allegedly a reflection of the command and wisdom of God. Just consider God's Law in the Torah.

Randal: Don't be too quick to dismiss the Torah. That ancient code makes impressive advances beyond other legal codes of the day. For example, in the Law of Hammurabi, if a man hits a pregnant woman and she loses the fetus, he needs to pay a fine, but if she dies, then his daughter (assuming he has one) is killed in retaliation.

Mia: Barbaric!

Randal: Yes, it is. The Torah addresses the same topic in Exodus 21:22-23. But in this case, the punishment is importantly different. Once again, the man must pay a fine if the woman loses the fetus, but if she dies, the text directs a payment of "life for life" (v. 23). In other words, the guilty party must accept the penalty as the perpetrator of the act. Punishment is not inflicted on an innocent third party.

Mia: That may be *less bad*, but that hardly makes it *good*. Like today, if some guy hits a woman and she falls on her stomach and miscarries, would you agree with *executing* the man in retaliation?

Randal: No, I'm not saying that. I was just pointing out that you should grant that the Torah constitutes a notable improvement in many ways over the other legal codes of the time.

Mia: Oh, I'm willing to grant that all day long. No problem there at all.

Randal: Wait, are you being sarcastic?

Mia: No, actually I'm being one hundred percent genuine. I truly have no problem recognizing that the Torah represents an incremental moral improvement over other legal codes of the day. That's precisely what we would expect from the long history of humanity: natural, incremental moral improvements.

But you, you're conceding that today we have moved beyond the moral improvement of the Torah since *you* wouldn't sanction killing a man in those circumstances. Put it this way: if there are two societies today which are identical except that in society 1 the man is executed in that circumstance while in society 2 he serves a sentence in prison, you would think society 2 is more just, all other things being equal, than society 1, right?

Randal: Yes, I agree with that.

Mia: Good, so to put it another way, the Torah may be *less* brutish than the Law of Hammurabi but that doesn't mean it isn't brutish.

Randal: "Brutish" is a strong word.

Mia: Don't worry, I'll be happy to expand on that. But first, I want to make sure that you agree on the fact that the authors of the Hebrew Bible do not appear to view the Torah in this very modest developmental way that you're proposing. The Torah isn't merely seen to be an advance on other ancient near eastern legal codes. Rather, biblical authors view it as a wonderful and gloriously wise revelation to order one's life and govern civil society.

Perhaps the fullest endorsement of the beauty and wisdom of the Law comes in Psalm 119 as the Psalmist exults in God's Law:

⁴ You have laid down precepts
  that are to be fully obeyed.
⁵ Oh, that my ways were steadfast
  in obeying your decrees!
⁶ Then I would not be put to shame
  when I consider all your commands.
⁷ I will praise you with an upright heart
  as I learn your righteous laws.
⁸ I will obey your decrees;
  do not utterly forsake me.

In verse after verse, the Psalmist captures the beauty of Torah culminating in the words of verse 160: "All your words are true; all your righteous laws are eternal."

Again, the Psalmist does not view the Torah merely as an incremental improvement in governance over the Law of Hammurabi. No, he views it as a glorious thing, a maximally wise way to order one's life. But we've already agreed that this isn't correct since the killing of a man for the inadvertent death of a fetus-in-utero is not justified and a civil society that didn't have that brutish penalty would, all other things being equal, be more humane and just than one that did.

But that's just the beginning: there are many other laws which pose an even sharper affront to our moral sensibilities.

Randal: Such as?

Mia: Let's start with the so-called Ordeal of the Bitter Waters.

Randal: Yikes, that sounds like a chapter from a fantasy novel.

Mia: Uh yeah, okay, this is probably not the time to make a joke. This is serious stuff. In Numbers 5:11-31 the Torah outlines what should happen to a woman who is suspected of adultery. The enraged hubby would drag her before the priest and she would be required to drink a bitter potion. Then, if her stomach swelled afterward she would be judged guilty of adultery.

I mean, I have enough problems with the notion of a jealous husband hiring a private investigator based on a hunch. Still, at least that guy might have a hope of getting some actual *evidence*. But who is to say why this poor woman's stomach might end up swelling? To subject her to this kind of trauma based potentially on nothing more than a possessive husband's gut feeling? And now her whole life might depend on how her body reacts to a particular concoction? Unconscionable!

Randal: Look, I'm not going to pretend that's anything other than awkward.

Mia: If you were to learn that Saudi Arabia today has a law like that on the books, would you merely call it *awkward?* Or would you say it is an affront to basic human rights and that it should be eradicated?

Randal: The latter, I suppose.

Mia: You 'suppose'? What a disappointingly understated response. Well, the next law may be even worse. In Deuteronomy 25:11-12 we read what should be done to a woman when she grabs a man's genitals while he is fighting her husband. Guess what? Her hand should be amputated, just lopped right off. I don't need to tell you that this was in a day before the mercy of general anesthesia.

Again, how would you react if you read that a judge in Saudi Arabia today decreed the amputation of a wife's hand for a similar action? Horrible, right?

Randal: Yes, I agree, I would respond viscerally in both cases. And it's definitely worse than just *awkward*.

Mia: I'm glad to hear that. But then you're already disagreeing sharply with the Psalmist who believes this law manifests God's glorious wisdom for regulating the self and civil society today. You don't think that applies today, clearly. But then what about ancient Israel? Did *they* get it wrong?

Randal: Well, I . . .

Mia: Actually, hold that thought. I want to pile on one more case and this one is probably the worst of all. Imagine for the moment that you read the following story in the news:

> (**Kabul, Afghanistan**) Yesterday, reports surfaced of a public stoning in the city of Saidu Sharif in the Swat Valley of eastern Afghanistan. Early reports identify two parents as presenting their thirteen-year-old son to public authorities for being "stubborn and rebellious". Town elders gathered together and stoned the boy until he was dead. The Al Qaeda held district of Swat has become notorious in recent months due to its enforcement of a strict Sharia law. (**Associated Press**)

I'm guessing that you would be shocked and morally indignant at this report. And I bet you'd denounce it as a moral atrocity, amirite?

Randal: I'm not going to sugarcoat it: that sounds abominable. I'd be horrified, disgusted . . .

Mia: And yet, you have a passage just like that in Deuteronomy 21:18-21, a passage in which parents are directed to take an insubordinate child to the elders to be stoned to death. This must surely be one of the most shocking passages of all in the Torah. But to really see how shocking it is, you need to listen to a Christian biblical scholar defending it. Just consider how Eugene Merrill addresses this passage. Merrill describes the steps under which the execution would take place with a disturbing matter-of-factness while making clear that according to verse 19, the child was definitely not yet an adult. Against that backdrop, Merrill then explains why it would be necessary to pelt this insubordinate youth to death with rocks. He writes:

> The severity of the punishment appears to outweigh the crime, but we must recognize that parental sovereignty was at stake. Were insubordination of children toward their parents to have been tolerated, there would have been but a short step toward the insubordination of all of the Lord's servant people to him, the King of kings.[7]

Did you catch that? Parental sovereignty is apparently at stake: that's why Merrill believes it was necessary to pelt the child to death with rocks. He's defending it as an *honor killing*.

Randal: Ouch, I agree that's an ugly justification all right. I remember reading about a contemporary honor killing in Canada a few years ago. A Muslim father in Toronto named Muhammad Parvez and his son together strangled his sixteen-year-old daughter to death because she refused to wear the hijab and conform to other rules in their conservative Muslim household.[8] Needless to say, I felt terrible for the poor daughter who was victim to the violence and cruelty of her father and his evil cultural assumptions.

Mia: Careful, it sounds like you might be saying there is a wicked ideology in the Bible. That's the surest path to theological exile in the Christian community.

Randal: I've thought a lot about this. I think any Christian who wrestles with these texts and who allows the compassion and mercy

---

[7] *Deuteronomy: An Exegetical and Theological Exposition of Holy Scripture* (B&H, 1994), 295.

[8] Bob Mitchell and Noor Javed, "I killed my daughter ... with my hands," *Toronto Star*, June 16, 2010, https://www.thestar.com/news/crime/2010/06/16/i_killed_my_daughter__with_my_hands.html

of their God-given moral intuitions to speak back to them will feel that they are out at sea, being tossed by waves in a churning storm. As they move deeper into the storm, the swells grow larger and they might begin to wonder if they'll ever make it to shore. That has often been my experience when I have carefully considered some of the violence of the Torah.

And so, let me now suggest that the way to get guided back to shore starts with finding that fixed point of light—the lighthouse, as it were—that will bring us in. Find the lighthouse and keep your eyes on it and you can find your way through the storm.

Mia: Wow, that's very dramatic. And the lighthouse is . . . ?

Randal: *Jesus*, of course!

Mia: Ah, I should've guessed.

Randal: I know it might sound like a cliché, but I'm deathly serious. Every Christian should recognize that Jesus is the interpretive key for the Bible. The entire Bible is about him and for him and to him, so we should always read the entire Bible in light of him.

Mia: Don't be offended, but it sounds like you're just piling up bumper-sticker maxims. How does this work out in these specific cases?

Randal: Well, first off, Jesus is the fulfillment of the Law (Matthew 5:17-20). If you want to know the true purpose of the Law, you must read it through Jesus.

To illustrate what I mean, bear with me while I give an illustration. Picture a husband and wife who live happily in a small one-bedroom suite. This couple loves living in the city: they regularly go to parties and clubs, they leave on a moment's notice and lock up the apartment to go on a vacation to the tropics; they work long but satisfying hours at their startup business; they are happy and fulfilled.

Then suddenly they give up their apartment and the life they enjoyed in the city and move to the suburbs where they buy a new home with a fenced yard near a school. They paint one bedroom with a Sesame Street motif and put in a crib, the husband builds a playset in the backyard, and they buy lots of toys and fill a closet with baby clothes.

Now what do you suppose explains all those perplexing changes?

Mia: Lemme guess: could it be that the wife is ... pregnant?

Randal: You got it! If we only considered their actions relative to their satisfying life in the city, all those changes would appear perplexing. But of course, they are all explained given the expectation of a pregnancy: that future child provides a perspective to make sense of all their otherwise perplexing actions.

I'm not suggesting the problem with the Bible can be interpreted just that neatly, but I am claiming that the basic logic is quite similar: we need to read the perplexing things that come before in light of Jesus who comes after. And so, when we have questions about Torah, we should look to Jesus as its fulfillment.

Mia: Fine, but how does *Jesus* explain all that?

Randal: Jesus said he came not to destroy the Law and Prophets but to fulfill them, in other words, to show their true meaning, end, and purpose. And clearly, that purpose wasn't to establish the one perfect way to govern society. Jesus was actually quite explicit about this when he noted in Matthew 19:3-9 that the Mosaic law on divorce was a concession to where the people were at rather than an expression of God's perfect will for all time. This opens up the space for recognizing *accommodation* in the Torah to the imperfect circumstances of human history.

Mia: Accommodation? You mean something like that idea of incremental moral improvement?

Randal: Yes. And so, insofar as the Psalmist didn't recognize the Law as an accommodation, insofar as he believed it was the maximally perfect final way to regulate oneself and civil society, to that degree he was wrong.

Mia: Wow, so the Psalmist made mistakes?

Randal: He didn't have the full picture. That only came with Jesus. I don't think that's revolutionary. God is inerrant in his actions in the writing of scripture. But that doesn't mean that the human author of Scripture is thereby inerrant in all *his* perspectives. You cited the lofty view of the Law in Psalm 119. I don't think that the Psalmist had the accommodationist picture that Jesus seems to take when he addresses divorce. But that doesn't negate the voice of the Psalmist. Rather, it should remind us that only God sees the *whole* picture. The final authority in all Scripture resides with God's voice in the text as it is interpreted through Jesus.

Psalm 119 is only the tip of the iceberg. The fact is that the Psalmist often says things that the Christian should disagree with. For example, in Psalm 37:13 he says that God laughs at the destruction of the wicked and their future judgment. And in Psalm 69:28 the Psalmist pleads that the names of his enemies would be removed from the Book of Life. The Psalmist says many other things about his enemies that are equally awful and inconsistent with what a Christian believes about God and proper holiness.

So why do we think differently from the Psalmist? Because Jesus explicitly said in Matthew 5:43-44 that while it has been said you should hate your enemy, he calls us to *love* our enemies. And where the Law called for a woman to be stoned for adultery, Jesus called for mercy (John 8:1-11).

The very heart of the Law, so Jesus said, is to love God and neighbor. That's what it is to be like Jesus. And as I already pointed out, the purpose of Scripture, as Paul says in I Timothy 3:14-17, is to make us more like Jesus. So what does that look like? Admittedly, it isn't always clear, but St. Augustine offered an excellent guiding principle when he suggested that we always ought to read the Bible so as to increase love of God and neighbor. Thus, if a reading of Scripture leads us away from that love, we need to reconsider that reading. I think that's great advice.

So while I don't have an explanation for everything, I do think there is clearly evidence of accommodation in the text, there is evidence of human weakness and fallibility—as in the Psalmist's angry outbursts—and we ought to read all of it in light of the person and life of Jesus who showed us the true heart of God the Father.

When people read the Torah as perfect in the unqualified sense suggested by Psalm 119 rather than as an incremental improvement indicative of divine accommodation but ultimately pointing toward Jesus as its fulfillment, I believe they misread it. And a good sign that they are misreading is that their way of reading does not increase love of God and neighbor. Their reading often forces them to justify imperfect legal dictates that, if consistently followed, could unfairly terrorize or inflict excessive violence on a wife, or perpetuate the most torturous death of a child. Their reading forces them into a cognitive dissonance with their basic moral intuitions as they recoil in disgust at honor killings or hand amputations carried out in other contexts.

Most people today recognize that those actions are wrong, so when Christians find themselves defending the trial of bitter waters, the amputation of hands, or the stoning of a child, I think they are thereby attempting to cauterize their moral compassion and sense of justice for the sake of their reading of the text. And that, I believe, is a mistake.

Mia: But isn't this all just a bit too neat and tidy? How do you defend yourself against the charge that you're just reading the Bible in light of your modern cultural assumptions?

Randal: First off, I don't think this is "neat and tidy" at all. It's messy. We have to read carefully and judiciously in light of God as revealed in Jesus, looking for moral development in the text, guided by readings that increase rather than decrease love of God and neighbor.

What is more, I'd say that objection can be turned right back onto the objector. We all read the Bible in light of our own beliefs. So-called modern cultural assumptions—such as the belief in the injustice and cruelty of hand amputation and stoning—are not thereby automatically more suspect than well-entrenched assumptions about the moral rightness of such actions.

Let me put it this way: the abolitionist movement of the nineteenth century was up against centuries of Christians reading the Bible as pro-slavery and yet we all know which side won that debate. I think it is reasonable to think Christians who categorically reject practices like honor killing and hand amputation are in a moral position analogous to the abolitionists.

One more thing: that hypothetical objector is just mistaken to think that these issues only became a matter of moral concern in the modern era. We can see Christians throughout history wrestling with the way to interpret biblical violence, to recognize development in the text, and with how to read the Hebrew Scriptures in light of the coming of Jesus.

The bottom line is this: Christians can disagree over how to interpret the Torah and the ethics and wisdom of its various laws. But no Christian should find herself compelled to sacrifice her conscience or to go against the way she believes God is revealed in Jesus for a particular reading of those passages. As Martin Luther famously said when he took his stand at the Council of Worms, "to go against conscience is neither right nor safe."

God has given us a conscience, and reading Scripture in light of Christ, ever guided in our pursuit of greater love of God and neighbor, we should not be afraid to use it.

7

⛵

How can you take Christian claims seriously when the universe is this large and old?

Mia: I'm a Mark Twain fan and to honor his skeptical legacy I'm going to introduce my next gripe by quoting a passage from the insatiable wit. And forgive him if he is off somewhat with his scientific timeline: he is writing in the nineteenth century, after all. But the main point comes through loud and clear:

> Man has been here 32,000 years. That it took a hundred million years to prepare the world for him is proof that that is what it was done for. I suppose it is. I dunno. If the Eiffel Tower were now representing the world's age, the skin of paint on the pinnacle-knob at its summit would represent man's share of that age; and anybody would perceive that that skin was what the tower was built for. I reckon they would, I dunno.[9]

---

[9] Mark Twain, *What is Man? And Other Philosophical Writings* (University of California Press, 1973), 106.

I love that quote. Twain plays it up with his aw shucks folksy charm and yet along the way he deals a death blow to the credibility of Christian claims.

Randal: It's a great image, I agree with that. And it's definitely folksy. But I don't see the death blow of which you speak. I take it your point is that Twain wants us to think Christianity and its revelatory claims are implausible?

Mia: Um, *yeah!* Twain is inviting you to contemplate how laughably *absurd* it is for human beings to conclude that they are important and that the earth is somehow the center of God's concern in this vast universe. The presumption of a skin of paint thinking the tower that came before was all made for the paint? Absurd. The presumption of a species thinking the eons that came before were all creating a universe made for it? Equally absurd.

Randal: Hmm, well actually I'm inclined to think the comparison of human beings and our privileged planet to a non-descript skin of paint is the most absurd thing of all.

Mia: Of course you do, O Mr. Christian master-of-deflection. I can tell that deep down that quote has disturbed you deeply. Well, I'm just getting started! While we've long been aware of the absurdity of claims to human uniqueness, the best criticism of that delusion may be found in Carl Sagan's book *Pale Blue Dot*.

Randal: Sagan? Why am I not surprised?

Mia: I know you Christians think Sagan, that revered popularizer of science and reason, spelled his name with a 'T', but don't demonize him just for speaking the truth. The title of the book refers to the way that the earth appeared in a famous picture taken by the Voyageur spacecraft in 1990. After more than a decade hurtling many times faster than a speeding bullet into the void, Voyageur turned its camera back around and snapped a picture of earth. And this humbling image, a blue-tinged pixel almost lost in a vast, unimaginably ancient backdrop, is the basis for Sagan's meditation. This is how he puts it:

> Look again at that dot. That's here. That's home. That's us. On it everyone you love, everyone you know, everyone you ever heard of, every human being who ever was, lived out their lives. The aggregate of our joy and suffering, thousands of confident religions, ideologies, and economic doctrines, every hunter and forager, every hero and coward, every creator and destroyer of civilization, every king and peasant, every young couple in love, every mother and father, hopeful child, inventor and explorer, every teacher of morals, every corrupt politician, every "superstar," every "supreme leader," every saint and sinner in the history of our species lived there—on a mote of dust suspended in a sunbeam.[10]

Sagan nails it. To put it bluntly, how can you take Christian claims seriously when the universe is this large and old?

Randal: Look, just to be clear, I don't think the guy is Satan. I have admiration for his writing: "a mote of dust suspended in a sunbeam"? Awesome stuff. He was a great communicator and a first-rate propagandist.

Mia: *Propagandist?* Omigosh, jealous much?

Randal: Hey, a propagandist is a person who promotes a particular cause. Sagan was definitely a major promoter of his own view of secularist freethought. If the shoe fits . . .

Mia: Based on what you said before, you're a propagandist. Or you *could* just call Sagan an apologist.

---

[10] Carl Sagan, *Pale Blue Dot: A Vision of the Human Future in Space* (New York: Ballantine, 1994), 6.

Randal: Fair enough, he was an apologist who dabbled in propagandistic rhetoric for the sake of freethought secularism.

Mia: No, no, no, you don't get away with that. Is it 'propaganda' when Christians talk about how life is surely meaningless *without* God because we'd be left to fend for ourselves in a cruel, mindless universe that cares nothing about us? Or is it only propaganda when the story is one *you* don't like?

Randal: Fine, fair point. Okay, he's an apologist: I'll leave it at that. And you're right: with his soaring description Sagan conveys to us a sense of our profound *insignificance* set against that staggeringly vast cosmic backdrop.

Mia: And he's not done, either. Having made these humbling observations, Sagan then seeks to drive the point home by emphasizing the implications that this has for our cosmic insignificance. He hammers the nail in the coffin like this:

> Our posturings, our imagined self-importance, the delusion that we have some privileged position in the Universe, are challenged by this point of pale light. Our planet is a lonely speck in the great enveloping cosmic dark. In our obscurity, in all this vastness, there is no hint that help will come from elsewhere to save us from ourselves.[11]

The message is simple: the miniscule size and insignificance of the earth lost in a universe of unimaginable size and scope supports the conclusion that there is no god, no special revelation, that we are truly alone. Sagan definitely makes religious notions of importance sound like the absurdity they are.

---

[11] Sagan, *Pale Blue Dot*, 7.

Randal: Hold on, the first thing to keep in mind is that Sagan isn't actually targeting Christianity.

Mia: Oh no?

Randal: No. If anything, he is targeting a claim known as *anthropocentrism* according to which the universe was created *for* human beings and we are at the center of the divine cosmic concern.

Mia: Wait a minute, isn't that *precisely* what you believe as a Christian? Don't you believe that human beings were made in the image of God and that Jesus died to save you?

Randal: Yes, but let's be clear here. I certainly believe that human beings are made in the image of God. However, Christianity does not explicitly require one to believe that human beings are the *only* creatures in the cosmos created in the image of God. For all we know, it is possible that there are other creatures with that status as well. That just isn't a topic addressed in Christianity.

And it is also worth noting that Christian theologians have taken a variety of perspectives on the relationship between the atoning death of Christ and his resurrection. Some believe that this single incarnation and resurrection is salvific for all creatures. That's my view.

But other theologians have speculated that if there are other civilizations on other planets that we know nothing about, God the Son might have died for them too. For example, the famous medieval theologian Thomas Aquinas actually considered the possibility of multiple incarnations.[12]

Mia: All that tells me is that there is no idea so crazy that some theologian hasn't thought of it, LOL.

---

[12] See Timothy Pawl, "Thomistic Multiple Incarnations," *Heythrop Journal*, 57, no. 2 (2016), 359-70.

Randal: That's a cheap shot. A moment ago, you were criticizing me because allegedly Christians never considered how a universe beyond our planet might fit into the divine plan. Now you criticize me when I point out that Christians were already wrestling with the question centuries ago.

Anyway, as I said, *I* don't subscribe to the view of multiple incarnations. Instead, I believe the incarnation of Jesus on planet earth alone was sufficient for the redemption of creation. But that brings me to my next point: the Christian Gospel of redemption isn't limited, as you suppose, to saving human beings. Rather, as Paul says in Colossians 1:15-20, it is God's plan to redeem *all things*, whether things on earth or things in heaven.

So to return for a second to John 3:16, I think Christians make a mistake when they assume that God so loved the world means only that God so loved *human beings*. I take it in the fullest sense: God so loved *the whole world*, that same world he created in the beginning, he loves it all.

Mia: Just planet earth, eh? No love for Venus or Mars?

Randal: Whoa, another cheap shot: you're on a roll. No, actually, 'world' here is a translation of the Greek word *cosmos*: in other words, the totality of creation. And that most surely includes Venus, Mars and yes, the whole universe.

In short, I think you are mistaken to assume that Christianity is committed to anthropocentrism. Some Christians do accept it in one form or another, but the beliefs that God created the universe for human beings and that human beings are the only creatures with God's image are simply not part of mere Christianity.

Mia: Fine, I won't quibble over that: I know better than to argue with Christians about what *real* Christianity is. I'd have more success nailing Jell-O to the wall.

Randal: That's another low blow.

Mia: Yeah, I know I shouldn't be so hard on Jell-O. But seriously, it's not worth debating. You've already made a claim that is no less extraordinary, namely that all salvation for the entire universe comes through this one incarnation of Jesus on planet earth. As you were making that claim, I thought of the XDF or 'eXtreme Deep Field' image that NASA released on September 25, 2012. It's a truly incredible picture, a photo composite of ten years of data drawn from the Hubble Space Telescope which was focused on the center of the Hubble Ultra Deep Field.

Perhaps even more mind-blowing, that extraordinary image, packed with over five thousand ancient galaxies up to 13 billion years old, was made from a miniscule one thirty-two millionth of the night sky. It gives us just a glimpse of the vast scope of our universe.

Randal: Wow, yeah, the universe is a vast place, all right. Twenty years ago astronomers believed there were approximately 100 billion galaxies in the known universe. Incredibly, that number has now expanded by a factor of 20 to over two trillion. And to think that a century ago, the only galaxy we knew was the Milky Way!

Who really knows how large the universe is? I suspect we can't begin to imagine.

Mia: Good, so I think we're on the same page. But that's what I don't get: you still want to suggest that this tiny planet is somehow at the center of God's redemptive action for this whole, vast universe? That it carries creatures with his unique creative stamp? That it is the place where brokenness and sin radiated out to distort all those trillions of galaxies? That it is the home of a plan of redemption for those 'sinful' galaxies?

I'm not saying the story is impossible. But good gosh, is it ever *implausible*! Like I said, Twain and Sagan nailed it.

Randal: Believe me, I can see where you're coming from. But I also want to point out that our sense of what is plausible should not be the last word on anything, not least because plausibility is something that is relative to each individual. My Christian claims may seem implausible to you, but atheism and naturalism are enormously implausible to me.

So we would all do well to keep an open mind. The world is endlessly surprising. And frankly, the claims of Christianity, including the fact that we are created in the image of God, that there was a fall, and that God is redeeming creation, all these claims are in my view, no more extraordinary on their face than the fact that the heavy oak chair we talked about earlier is composed of vibrating packets of energy.

Mia: This isn't just an oak chair. Salvation starting right *here* on planet earth? Come on, man.

Randal: Hey, it had to start somewhere, so *why not* here? I'm reminded of the old 1980s movie *Red Dawn*. In the movie, the United States is taken over by the Soviets. Now imagine that something like that really happened . . .

Mia: Okay, but the Soviet empire is history: these days it would more likely be the Chinese.

Randal: Fine, okay, so one day, Chinese soldiers invade and take over the country and the American government and military retreat to Canada to regroup while governing in exile from Ottawa.

In this scenario, you live in a little town, Podunk North Dakota. And while you're up late one night studying Mandarin, you hear a commotion in the wheatfield. You run out and see an Apache helicopter landing and two soldiers and the President of the United States emerging from the cornfield and they're running toward *your* house.

You can bet nobody would ever have imagined that the plan to retake America would begin in *your* cornfield just outside Podunk North Dakota. And yet, here we are. In the next few minutes you learn that the government is launching an all-out offensive against the Chinese occupiers and it begins *right here in Podunk.*

It seems to me that the story of Christianity is a lot like that: an average planet orbiting an average star in an average galaxy in an average supercluster of galaxies: basically, Podunk North Dakota. And yet, from these humble beginnings a story is radiating out of God retaking his entire universe.

And here's the most incredible part: we have a front-row seat.

8

⛵

How did Adam and Eve turn
T-Rex into a predator?

Mia: Retaking the universe? Oh my, how grand! But my withering sarcasm provides a great segue to my next question. Because, see, I'm not at all persuaded that the universe needs to be 'retaken' in the first place.

To make my point, let's consider one particular Christian doctrine and probe it a bit against this dizzying cosmic backdrop. I'm thinking of the fall, and in particular the idea that sin and evil came into the world through the immoral actions of two primordial human beings, Adam and Eve.

Randal: I see, so you want to know how Adam and Eve brought about effects extending to the range of the Hubble Deep Field and the XDF?

Mia: I *could* ask you about that, but I won't be that cruel! Instead, I'll cut you a break and be content if you can at least explain things here on planet earth. In the Christian story, God created a perfect world and then two naked human beings ate from the wrong fruit tree and screwed it all up.

That sounds like a classic myth, a story that you tell around the campfire. The problem is that it doesn't seem to resonate at all with what we know of earth history from science. Homo sapiens only appeared in the last few hundred thousand years, at the tail end of an earth history extending over four billion years. That history has seen death and carnivores, predators and parasites all for hundreds of millions of years before we ever appeared on the scene. Needless to say, it doesn't make sense, man.

Hey, here's a concrete example for you to 'chew' on. Paleontologists have discovered fossilized dung from Tyrannosaurus-Rex which includes Triceratops frill: in other words, chewed up bits of Triceratops. So we know that T-Rex was a ravenous killer millions of years before humans appeared on the scene. But in Genesis 3:14-20 we read that the fall of creation, including all this death and predation and suffering, is somehow the result of the sins of Adam and Eve. So I'll make this simple for you: just explain to me how Adam and Eve can possibly be held responsible for T-Rex. I don't need to hear about the Hubble Deep Field. Just explain that scary meat-eating reptilian predator. How did two human beings eating a piece of forbidden fruit in a garden turn T-Rex into a fearsome Jurassic Park exhibition?

Randal: First off, I agree that many Christians live with an uncomfortable cognitive dissonance on this question. They may be critical of young earth creationism, as I am, but they've never taken the time to consider how *they* should think about death and the fall.

So let's start with one specific attempt to take the bull by the horns. William Dembski approached the problem like this:

> To make us realize the full extent of human sin, God does not merely allow personal evils (i.e. the disordering of our souls and the sins we commit as a result) to run their course subsequent to the Fall. In

addition, God allows natural evils (e.g. death, predation, parasitism, disease, drought, floods, famines, earthquakes, and hurricanes) to run their course prior to the Fall. Thus, God himself wills the disordering of creation, making it defective on purpose.[13]

Mia: Wait, wut? Let me get this straight: you're saying that God made T-Rex a predator on purpose? *Why?* What is the causal mechanism that would explain this? How is it that the actions of two people in a garden could ever *cause events millions of years before those human beings even existed?* It doesn't make any sense.

Randal: Yeah, well, according to Dembski, God creates foreknowing how human beings will act and he builds a response to their future sinful actions into creation from the beginning. And so, even though T-Rex came first, it was created from the beginning as a predator in response to God's foreknowledge of the future actions of Adam and Eve.

Mia: Huh? I must admit that I don't even understand what you're saying. The point of T-Rex-the-predator is somehow to get human beings to figure out that *we're* sinful? Is this not like the most ineffective and gratuitous way to communicate a message in the history of the universe? How is it justified to make a T-Rex that will eat a Triceratops seventy million years ago so that we can discover a bit of its fossilized dung today and thereby be led to contemplate our own sinfulness?

And what about the fact that for every lump of fossilized T-Rex dung we find that has Triceratops frill, there are millions of piles that decayed into nothing and disappeared forever? How did *that* serve to inform us of human sinfulness?

I'm sorry to break this to you, but *no explanation is better than a crazy one*. And this is definitely crazy. I think you should've just played your mystery card and left it at that.

---

[13] Dembski, *The End of Christianity: Finding a Good God in an Evil World* (Nashville: B&H, 2009), 145.

Randal: Personally, I'm not a fan of Dembski's proposal but I just thought it was worth mentioning. Myself, I'd be inclined to approach the matter differently by cutting the Gordian knot altogether.

Mia: What do you mean?

Randal: I suspect we should stop trying to draw any concrete causal link between human actions and physical death in creation.

Mia: Translation, please.

Randal: I don't think we should try to say that these specific actions by these human beings directly *caused* these results in nature. Another way to look at the fall narrative is that it communicates the universal fact of our need for redemption by telling a story of cosmic import.

Mia: I'm still not following you. Are you saying that maybe there wasn't a fall? That it really is *just a campfire story* like I said?

Randal: Well, the same points that we've been considering about earth history generally can be applied back to the history of Homo sapiens. Many Christians accept Neo-Darwinian evolutionary theory and they believe God created in accord with those processes. Nor is this a new development: Christians have been defending that view since Darwin first proposed his theory.[14]

Mia: So you accept evolution?

Randal: I'm not a biologist but I have seen a lot of evidence in favor of common ancestry and for evolutionary change over time.

---

[14] See David Livingstone, *Darwin's Forgotten Defenders: The Encounter Between Evangelical Theology and Evolutionary Thought* (Vancouver: Regent College Publishing, 1984).

I don't tie my theology to Neo-Darwinian evolutionary theory but I have reconciled my theology to it.

Mia: You've 'reconciled'? So benevolent! Have you 'reconciled' to the theory of gravity as well?

Randal: Hey, Mia, if you keep insulting me, people will think I have a severe inferiority complex.

Mia: Maybe you do. So then how *do* you explain the fall? What's the point?

Randal: I think Genesis 3 may best be interpreted as myth. By 'myth' I *don't* mean something fake or false as in the popular phrase "just a myth". Rather, I mean a particular story that conveys a universal truth in narrative form.

Mia: And what's that 'truth'?

Randal: Creation is not what it should be. Whether that fact is tied to a historical primordial fall or simply the fact that creation has not yet achieved the ends for which God has purposed it since the beginning, the fact remains that it needs God's healing, redemptive hand before it achieves its final purpose. And I do believe that that will include God healing not only human beings but also the problems of predation, carnivory, and parasitism: in other words, everything that Paul refers to as the 'groaning' of creation (Romans 8:19-23).

Mia: Until the lion lies down with the lamb? Is that the idea? T-Rex also needs to become a vegetarian?

Randal: I wrote an entire chapter on carnivores in heaven in my book *What on Earth Do We Know About Heaven?* I think there will be redemption for non-human creatures but it will involve the healing of those aspects of their nature that involve them inflicting suffering on others.

Mia: Okay, well, you set yourself up for this last question: if Genesis 3 is a myth, then why isn't Jesus likewise a myth?

Randal: That's easy. First off, if you have a collection of diverse documents like we have in the Bible, the fact that you may have misread one passage as historical doesn't automatically mean that you've misread all the others.

Second point: in the case of the Gospels, those are clearly written in the style of Greco-Roman biographies: they are *histories* through and through so there's no doubt about the genre.

And one more thing: the fact that a story is a myth does not mean it fails to convey objective facts. Even if the narrative of Genesis 3 is a myth in the sense I described, it nonetheless conveys the objective fact of universal alienation from God and with it the fact that all creation needs a real redeemer. And that's who Jesus is.

9

⛵

If theology is true then
why is it always changing in light of science?

Mia: Hey, let's keep talking about theology and science for a bit more. You see, I think the problem here is a lot bigger than you are ready to recognize. I can set up my question with a couple of quotes. The great science popularizer Neil deGrasse Tyson says: "I have yet to see a successful prediction about the physical world that was inferred or extrapolated from the content of any religious document."[15] Lawrence Krauss echoed the point in a dialogue with Richard Dawkins where he observed:

> I've challenged theologians to give me a single example of a contribution to human knowledge that theology has provided in the last 500 years, and when I talk to major theologians, and I do, believe it or not, the answer I always get is, What do you mean by

---

[15] Cited by John Loftus in John Loftus and Randal Rauser, *God or Godless: One Atheist. One Christian. Twenty Controversial Questions* (Grand Rapids, MI: Baker, 2013), 117.

knowledge? And I point out, as I talk to biologists, or a historian, or a psychologist, I get concrete answers, they give me this epistemological . . . anyway.[16]

Randal: I hear those kinds of statements a lot from atheists.

Mia: I'm not surprised, because they make an important point, and one that is rather embarrassing for the theologian. If I can put it this way: the relationship between theology and science isn't a two-way street. Rather, it is always one way with science advancing and theology forever beating a hasty retreat.

In his famous poem "Dover Beach," the 19th century poet Matthew Arnold described the advance of science against the sea of religion, theology, and faith by referring to the "melancholy, long, withdrawing roar": as science forever advances, theology forever retreats. The picture, in short, supports the conclusion that nature is all that exists and theology doesn't have anything interesting to say about it that can't be said better from the perspective of science.

So I guess I would put the question like this: if theology is true then why is it always changing in light of science? Why doesn't it ever go in the other direction.

Randal: That's a fair question. First, I'd like to return to those quotes from Tyson and Krauss. I definitely don't want to leave them hanging because I think there are some deep errors in their thinking that need to be addressed directly.

Tyson says that 'religious documents' do not successfully predict aspects of the physical world. The comment assumes that the *point* of religious documents is to predict aspects of the world, as if they are in direct competition with natural science. But that's ridiculous.

Mia: So no religious documents make claims about nature?

---

[16] Krauss/Dawkins Dialogue, https://vialogue.wordpress.com/2012/02/26/something-from-nothing-notes-review-response/

Randal: Hold on, that brings me to my second point: I'm not actually interested in a general discussion about 'religious documents'. Tyson speaks in unqualified and hopelessly broad terms about religious documents generally as if there is this one standard by which we should judge them all. But the fact is that religion is a vastly diverse subject matter and the range of documents that can be identified as religious is equally vast and diverse. To suggest that they should all be held up to a single standard is just silly. That just shows the rhetorical lack of discipline with secularists like Tyson.

Mia: Picky picky picky! Okay, maybe Tyson should have specified *the Bible*. Would you be happy with that? So let's just pose the question again: when did the *Bible* ever make a prediction that was vindicated by natural science?

Randal: Who said the Bible makes scientific predictions in the first place?

Mia: A lot of Christians do.

Randal: As you may guess from what I've said so far, I think that's a big mistake. Every time Christians try to marry their reading of the Bible with the science of the day, they are setting themselves up to be a widower because the science will eventually change and when it does, it will leave the theology that was grafted onto it in tatters.

Mia: Careful, you're mixing your marriage and textile metaphors. And, if that's really the case then why are theologians always *trying* to graft their theology onto science? Did they not get your memo? And to take up Krauss' point, why don't you see science doing the same thing? But no, it's always a one way street, science making bold advances in its understanding of nature while theology rides the coattails.

Randal: Is that how you see it? Let me frame that for you a little differently. Systematic theology is an integrative discipline. What the theologian is attempting to do is take Christian scripture as interpreted through, and thereby informed by specific traditions, and interpret it all in light of one's logical reasoning, moral reasoning, personal and communal experience, and the best *Wissenschaft* of the day.

Mia: 'Wissenschaft'?

Randal: The best knowledge of the day, including natural science.

Mia: Well then, just *say that* and spare us your pretentious words.

Randal: Okay then, well, natural science doesn't do that with respect to theology because it is simply *a different kind of project*. It is *not* an interdisciplinary project that seeks to provide a unifying framework across multiple disciplines. Rather, it is a focused inquiry into the structure and processes of nature. That explains the asymmetry. So of course theologians will end up appealing to the results of science in their theologizing while scientists won't appeal to theologians: one field is integrative and interdisciplinary as it seeks to relate Christian doctrine to the best learning of the age whereas the other inquiry is a focused investigation into nature. They are simply different disciples with different fields of inquiry.

Mia: Erm . . .

Randal: You look skeptical.

Mia: Hey, how'd you know? You're a mind-reader!

Randal: Not that impressive since you're in *my* mind.

Mia: Yeah, well the thing is, if scientists suddenly started appealing to God in their scientific theories, somehow I don't think you'd be unhappy about it.

Randal: I don't know what you mean by "appealing to God . . ."

Mia: For example, God as an explanation for the Big Bang.

Randal: Oh, they're free to do that and I won't complain if they do. The point, however, is that when they do so they are not doing it as a *scientist* but rather as a *philosopher* or a *theologian*. In other words, at that point, they'd be leaving science proper by attempting to interpret their scientific findings in light of a particular theology or philosophy. And many scientists actually *do* that. Some of them, like Paul Davies, explore conceptions of God far from Christian theism. Others like Stephen Hawking deny theism outright. And still others, like R.J. Russell, work from within an explicitly Christian context. But whatever their specific views, the second they move from nature to *God and nature*, they've moved from science proper to the interdisciplinary field of theology and science.

Mia: I think that you're talking around Krauss' point. I assume you're going to agree that science has made many contributions to knowledge in the last 500 years. So let me ask you directly: what is a single example of a contribution to human knowledge in the last 500 years that has come from theology? Come on, just one thing will do!

Randal: When you quoted Krauss making that point, you went on to quote him observing that theologians reply to his question by asking what he *means* by knowledge.

Mia: Yeah, and he clearly took that as a dodge . . . which it most definitely is.

Randal: Not at all: you're not *dodging* a question when you ask for clarification as to what it *means*. On the contrary, Krauss is the one dodging if he refuses to explain what he means by knowledge.

The fact is that the concept of knowledge is a complex one. Some philosophers define it as 'justified true belief' but many others critique that definition. And if even the basic definition of knowledge is controversial, you can bet that it is controversial to speak in the loosey goosey way that Krauss seems to prefer.

Mia: So you're saying a person has to be a professional philosopher just to ask the question?

Randal: No, I wasn't saying that. But I *was* saying that the word 'knowledge' can be defined in different ways, so if Krauss is going to make a stipulation about knowledge he does owe us some kind of definition.

If knowledge is a form of justified true belief then there are many facts that I believe are theological in nature which have been clarified in the last five hundred years such as facts about the nature of God's justification of sinners, increased conceptual clarity on the divine attributes, a better grasp of viable theories of the Trinity and so on.

Mia: Hold on, are you claiming that everyone agrees with those 'facts'?

Randal: No. And are *you* saying everyone must agree on a particular fact for it to constitute a contribution to human knowledge? Because there are people today who still deny that the earth is a sphere. You don't believe the mere existence of flat-earthism entails that the sphericity of the earth is not currently a contribution to human knowledge, do you?

Mia: No, of course not.

Randal: Well, that's precisely why Krauss needs to explain what *he* means. If a consensus of some sort is required for a truth-claim to constitute a contribution to knowledge then what type of consensus is required? If it isn't universal, what is it?

That question is actually quite complicated so I can see why Krauss didn't try to explain what he meant by a contribution to human knowledge. But that doesn't mean he can get away without explaining what he means. The question might sound meaningful and function effectively as an applause line for a secular and anti-religious audience. But there's nothing more to be said for it until someone explains what Krauss means.

10

⚓

How could a good God punish people through natural disasters?

Mia: Our conversation about science got me thinking about COVID-19. I sure am glad we can count on scientists to come up with a vaccine when terrible pandemics arise.

Randal: Agreed. I'm grateful for science.

Mia: So did you hear that some preachers have said that COVID-19 is God's judgment?

Randal: Yes, I did. I don't have time for those self-appointed prophets.

Mia: Well, maybe you're dismissing them too quickly. Did you notice that New Orleans was hit by a wave of COVID-19 right after they held Mardi Gras? Maybe COVID-19 is God's punishment for 'sinful' festivals like that. What do you think?

Randal: I don't buy that.

Mia: Hey, not so fast. I'm just getting started. How about hurricanes, earthquakes, plagues, or droughts? The Bible has a long history of linking natural disasters with divine judgment. And with no clear Biblical evidence that God has declared a moratorium on the practice, the question must be asked: does God *still* punish people through natural disasters today like he did in the good ole Bible days? You may think these wanna-be prophets are wrong but really, how do you know? Could they possibly be right?

Randal: My short answer is 'no.' But, I have a feeling that you're not going to be satisfied with a short answer.

Mia: How right you are. I'd like a direct answer to the question, thank you very much: how could a good God punish people through natural disasters?

And I do assume that you think God is good, *perfectly* good, as well as all-powerful and all-knowing. After all, you seemed to endorse all those attributes courtesy of the God of the Philosophers. So if God is all those things, how could he ever punish his poor human creatures in this wanton, cruel manner? And how do we know he isn't doing it to us now with every tortured breath and debilitating ache inflicted by a dreaded pandemic?

Randal: Since this isn't going to be a quick answer, I can see, let's be clear on what we're talking about. You've already given a decent working definition of God with which I agree: God is omnipotent, omniscient, and omnibenevolent or perfectly good.

But let's get clear on our other definitions. How would you define 'natural disasters'?

Mia: When I refer to natural disasters, I am thinking not of limited events that have discrete effects like a single lightning bolt striking a particular individual. Those are bad, sure, but I'm thinking of big, sprawling, random events and processes that affect potentially hundreds, thousands, or even millions of human beings and countless other sentient creatures: for example, a devastating flood or an earthquake and tsunami or a scorching heat wave . . .

Randal: Or a global pandemic.

Mia: Yes, exactly.

Randal: Okay, so there is one more thing we should clarify before diving into the question and that's the issue of punishment. Would you agree that punishment is the act of imparting a penalty to an individual for an offense committed?

Mia: That'll work for me. So my core claim is that God would not punish people by way of natural disasters. It just doesn't seem fair. It's too messy. And it sure isn't compassionate.

Randal: I actually agree with you on that. I've thought about this quite a bit. For me, the problems start with the fact that I believe God—a being who is indeed all-powerful, all-knowing, and all-good—would employ modes of punishment that discriminate the guilty from the innocent while restricting punishment to the former. An ethical punishment is, by definition, one that discriminates the guilty from the innocent.

Mia: Turns out I'm agreeing with you so far. What a surprise!

Randal: Good, I'll keep going then. Next, it also seems to me that a punishment must be *proportional*. Here the idea is that God would adjust the intensity of punishment relative to the culpability of the individuals being punished. So, for example, he would punish a person more severely if they were more culpable and he would punish a person less severely if they were less culpable.

Mia: Certainly, I agree with that, too. But then, you have a big problem, I think. The Bible often describes God punishing human populations through natural disasters and yet those natural disasters do not have that discrimination and proportionality that you agreed is essential for just punishments.

Natural disasters are almost by definition indiscriminate and disproportionate in their effects. The very complex and random nature of these events means that there is no clear pattern in which they afflict the guilty and spare the innocent. Nor is there any evidence that the degree of suffering that they create is commensurate to some degree of guilt on the part of each one of the specific persons who suffer as a result of the 'punishment.' When a tornado hits a town in Oklahoma, it may very well destroy the church run-homeless shelter while sparing the crack house next door. That deadly respiratory virus kills the devout Christian wife but spares her irreverent atheistic husband. Debris from the earthquake buries an infant but spares her negligent mother. Random casualties litter the landscape and there is just no rhyme or reason to any of it.

You're the one who believes that God punishes people in at least some of these natural disasters. So how do you make sense of any of that?

Randal: It is certainly *possible* that God could punish people by natural disasters in a way that discriminates between the guilty and innocent parties while correlating proportional suffering relative to the degree of guilt incurred. But I also agree that there really isn't evidence that he does do this.

A person could say, however, that this fact itself is evidence that God doesn't judge people this way any longer even though he *did* do so in the past. In other words, natural disasters don't discriminate in this fashion today but that doesn't mean they didn't do so during the past biblical events where God is described as acting in a punitive fashion through natural disasters.

Mia: Not so fast, bud. Where is there *any* evidence that natural disasters in biblical times discriminated between the guilty and innocent in this fashion? On the contrary, the opposite appears to be the case. Noah's flood drowned every land-dwelling organism except for Noah's family and his menagerie. That doesn't sound very fair, does it? What did other animals do to justify their being drowned? What did infants and small children do? What about the mentally handicapped? And yet, God drowned *everybody* just the same. It's the very *definition* of indiscriminate punishment.

But let me guess what your response will be: the go-to of many Christians is to say that because of the sin of Adam, we're all terrible human beings worthy of death anyway, so however it shakes down, God is justly punishing whomever gets hurt. I mean, basically, that's the get-out-of-jail free card for God. Whatever terrible thing befalls us, you can always say that human beings are all maximally sinful anyway because of Adam so whatever happens, it is automatically justified. Or does that not work with your claim that the Genesis 3 fall could be viewed as a myth?

Randal: Whether the fall was precisely historical or not, it is worth noting that Christians disagree about whether original sin includes the imputation of Adam's moral guilt so that human beings are *born guilty* or whether it only entails the transmission of the distorting impact of sin such that humans are born innocent but with a distorted nature that will inevitably result in personal sin.

Personally, I don't think original sin includes the imputation of Adam's guilt and so, for that reason, I don't think that everyone is automatically guilty and so properly subject to whatever horrors might befall them. Instead, I think that we are all *predisposed to sin* but that each of us actualizes our own specific sins and it is for our own specific sins that each of us is culpable.

Mia: Do you make this stuff up as you go along? Like seriously, a little while ago when we were talking about animal suffering, you said that you tend to view Genesis 3 as a myth, a story that communicates a universal truth of brokenness and sin. But now you say that 'Adam' is the source of original sin? How can a myth be the source of anything?

Randal: That's a perfectly fair question, although it would be better without the snark. What I'm saying is that whether or not there was a historical Adam, what the story of the fall conveys, in my view, is the universal brokenness of all humanity and our collective need for redemption. We are not born with the guilt of another person credited to us, but we are born with an inevitable predisposition to sin which will inevitably become a reality as we develop into moral agents.

Mia: Fair enough, I guess. Anyway, I want to keep my eye on the main topic. So if I may continue with a survey of terrible events, we can turn to the plagues of Egypt at the time of the Exodus. Those are a series of natural disasters and they befall an entire population from the house of Pharaoh straight on down to the most marginal peasants. Granted, the Israelites were sparred but you can't tell me that every single Egyptian was equally guilty. And the last plague involves killing the firstborn son of every family, again ranging from the house of Pharaoh straight on down to the squalid hovel of the poorest peasant.

Why would God kill a peasant's son? What could that poor little child have done that was worthy of that action?

Actually, come to think of it, maybe your tangent could be useful here. You see, if those peasant children are not automatically guilty because of Adam's sin then there is no obvious reason why they should be subject to this horrific judgment. On the contrary, surely they should have been spared.

And I'm warning you: don't play that "It was different in Bible times" card. Punishing vast populations indiscriminately is wrong now and it was wrong then, and you know it.

Randal: Actually, I suggested a formal grammar of punishment so there is no point in attacking me as if I'm the enemy. I do have something more I'd like to say, but first I want to clarify whether you believe punishment needs something more than discrimination and proportionality. Is that all you think is required?

Mia: That's a good question. I guess I would also think that the punishment should be *understood* by the person being punished.

Imagine, for example, that Billy steals a cookie from the cookie jar. His parents observe his deceptive action but they say nothing. Then, six months later, Billy's parents suddenly inform him that he cannot watch any television or play video games for the day. Billy's parents intend this prohibition as punishment for Billy's deception six months earlier, but *they never tell him their actions are punishment for his deception.*

This seems completely wrong. It would be wrong for Billy's parents to punish him *without explaining what the punishment was for.* The reason is that proper punishment requires that the one being punished understand the link between his or her indiscretion and the resulting punishment. So I think that proper punishment includes not only discrimination and proportionality but also *awareness.*

If this is true then surely it would follow that God would employ modes of punishment that *unambiguously* link the punishment to the offense. Doing so is important for deterrence, reformation, and punition. However, natural disasters *lack the interpretive context necessary for proper punishment.* Apart from the occasional alleged prophet who may provide an interpretive context to a relatively small subset of the affected population, there is no clear link between a specific natural disaster and some particular act requiring punishment.

And one more thing: given that punishment ought to be proportional to the offense it should never be cruel or unusual. I hope we can agree on that as well.

Randal: Yeah, cruel punishment is, by definition, disproportionate.

Mia: Good, but then here is your problem: if the suffering that is produced by natural disasters were classified as punishment, much of it would surely be categorized as *cruel and unusual.* Consider the 2017 flood in Houston which unfolded as a result of Hurricane Harvey. From elderly people in a retirement home slumped over in their wheelchairs, waist-deep in fetid, sewage-laced water to terrified children being pulled to their watery grave in a raging current, the suffering produced by the floods in Texas is anything but a proportional response to an offense.

Whether it is the cruelty of the flood of Hurricane Harvey or the flood of Genesis 6, I would ask you to imagine what it would be like to *punish* people by way of drowning. Back at the height of the controversy over water-boarding as a means of interrogation, Christopher Hitchens submitted himself to be water-boarded—a process that simulates drowning—to see if it really qualifies as cruel and unusual punishment. The memorable article he wrote of his experience was titled "Believe Me, It's Torture." It is worth quoting his account at some length:

> In this pregnant darkness, head downward, I waited for a while until I abruptly felt a slow cascade of water going up my nose. Determined to resist if only for the honor of my navy ancestors who had so often been in peril on the sea, I held my breath for a while and then had to exhale and—as you might expect—inhale in turn. The inhalation brought the damp cloths tight against my nostrils, as if a huge, wet paw had been suddenly and annihilatingly clamped over my face. Unable to determine whether I was breathing in or out, and flooded more with sheer panic than with mere water, I triggered the pre-arranged signal and felt the unbelievable relief of being pulled upright and having the soaking and stifling layers pulled off me. I find I don't want to tell you how little time I lasted.[17]

---

[17] Hitchens,"Believe Me, It's Torture," *Vanity Fair* (July 2, 2008), https://www. vanityfair.com/news/2008/08/hitchens200808

Now, to return to one of the tragedies of Hurricane Harvey, if you dare, try to imagine the experience of four small children and their great-grandparents being pulled under those swift-moving flood-waters. Or try to imagine millions of human beings and animals being drowned in an act of global divine retribution. Is there any condition under which such deaths could be considered a just divine punishment?

Randal: I agree that the Christian faces a dilemma here. And I think that many Christians live with a sort of cognitive dissonance at points like this. They recoil at the very suggestion of natural disasters today being divine judgment and yet they accept without a blink that seemingly random disasters which are equally indiscriminate and lacking in proportionality appear regularly in the Bible.

But to turn to your point about awareness, Christians commonly believe one thing was clear in the Bible: people were indeed aware of what they were being punished for. After all, they had prophets to tell them.

Mia: Prophets? It is far from obvious, at least in a vast number of circumstances that that was, in fact, the case. Consider again Noah's flood as an example. Assuming that the Noahic flood occurred as described, there is *no evidence* that the vast majority of human beings who would have been drowned throughout the globe would have ever known that there is a specific reason they were being drowned. After all, they didn't have access to Genesis 6-9 for an interpretive context and there's no evidence that they all received a special revelation as they were about to be drowned.

Randal: Okay, but in fairness, a person can always claim that these people *must* have received such a revelation. Though I admit that I prefer not to add wholly gratuitous *ad hoc* propositions into my theories.

Mia: Glad to hear that!

Randal: And while various biblical prophets may have offered warnings about other events—droughts, floods, earthquakes, and the like —I agree that there is no evidence that every person who suffered as a result of these disasters had the same clear revelation by which they could interpret their suffering.

Mia: Right, so in the vast majority of cases, it would seem that biblical punishments end up looking like suddenly smacking a child because of some action they did last week: the punishment is completely disconnected from the specific offense. So that's the awareness problem in a nutshell: what do you say in reply?

Randal: Well, for starters, a person could always reject those criteria by claiming that God has a unique status as creator and sustainer of all things such that those criteria simply don't apply to God when God punishes. Basically, he doesn't have to play by our rules. While I think there is some truth in that response, I also fear the danger of that move is that eventually the concept of punishment as we understand it becomes nearly meaningless as it is almost completely untethered from standard usage. So I don't want to go that route.

Mia: A wise move!

Randal: For that reason, I will proceed on the assumption that punishment means approximately the same thing whether the person doing the punishing is human or divine. And with that in mind, the same criteria must be in place: discrimination, proportionality, and awareness.

Mia: Great. And so . . . ?

Randal: And so one response would be to take an antirealist stance toward these descriptions.

Mia: Come again?

Randal: 'Antirealist' means that one would interpret those descriptions in a non-literal fashion: that is, God did not literally *punish* people in that manner.

Mia: Oooh, once again it sounds like you're traipsing onto dangerous ground for a good evangelical Christian. God didn't *actually* say what God *clearly said*? Keep going! I want to see how much trouble you get into on this one.

Randal: I get that. The idea can give people a jolt at first. But I've already given a few jolts to good evangelical Christians so hopefully they'll be getting used to it by now.

The key is to recognize that the basic idea I am proposing is more familiar and thus far less revolutionary than it sounds at first blush. When we were talking earlier you highlighted the gap between the description of the God of the Philosophers and the God of Abraham, Isaac, and Jacob. And I tried to show that theologians have good reasons for reading the Bible in the ways they do because they draw on several sources when interpreting the Bible including their intuitions, their logical reasoning, and their experience.

All of that can lead to a perfectly defensible portrait of God, one that is quite different from the description written down on at least some pages of the Bible. In particular, it can mean that the theologian ends up concluding that various actions attributed to God within the biblical narrative did not occur as described.

That's why theologians can argue that the God who regularly exhibits emotions—sometimes warm and tender and sometimes positively volcanic—is in fact impassible (that is, that he experiences no changes of emotional state); that's why they can say that the God who is described as having a body and sitting on a throne is, in fact, a non-physical substance that utterly transcends space; that's why they can say that the God who is described as regularly acting and reacting to human actions and events in the warp and woof of history in fact, utterly transcends time; that's why they can say that the God who is described as learning and changing his mind and having regrets actually knows all facts necessarily and from eternity.

Mia: I see, so this is another case where you're going to say the theologian's "vibrating packets of energy" differs radically from the heavy oak chair we sit on every day?

Randal: Possibly so. In all these cases, theologians appeal to the concept of *accommodation* which I mentioned earlier when discussing the way God is revealed progressively through the Law. According to that concept God speaks to finite human beings in terms and categories that we can grasp. God met the ancient Israelites as if he were like a human agent acting in history, but God is not merely another human agent. And it would also appear that God accommodated to the legal and ethical systems of the ancient Israelites while eventually moving them to the fullest revelation in Jesus.

Mia: Fine, but how does that apply to the judgment bit?

Randal: The ancient Israelites and other ancient peoples did not have a conception of nature such as we have today as in a discrete, autonomous sphere governed by natural laws which can be systematically investigated by the natural sciences. Instead, they tend to envision the processes of creation as manifesting an immediate expression of the divine will. As Psalm 104 eloquently puts it, it is God who waters the earth, feeds the plants, makes the grass grow, guides the sun and the moon, and even determines the course of the flow of water. All of these events and processes that we would understand today as being explicable in terms of nature were interpreted in ancient Israel as immediate expressions of the divine will.

When you have no distinct concept of nature as an autonomous realm of regularities that unfold independently of the immediate will of a (divine) agent, then it isn't surprising that you will *naturally* also explain natural disasters as an expression of that will: when nature is kind, God is benevolently disposed toward us and when nature is violent and cruel, God is punishing us.

Mia: So you're saying that God accommodated to the ancient Israelite view of nature, that he allowed them to think he was blessing and punishing them when, in fact, those were simply the events of nature that the Israelites errantly interpreted as the divine will?

Randal: Well, we've already seen Christian theologians insist that accommodation can justify reading descriptions of God's emotional life, his physical embodiment, his temporal location in space, and his developing knowledge figuratively. We have also seen reason to believe that he accommodated to imperfect understandings of justice in his revelation of the Law. It seems to me that the moral concerns you've raised about the literal interpretation of natural disasters as punishment at least warrants a serious consideration of an accommodation approach to these passages as well.

Mia: I'm listening to you closely and I didn't hear you say you actually *believe* this. I just heard you saying it should be considered as a possibility. Are you hedging your bets?

Randal: Hedging? Not exactly. But I don't think I have to endorse any particular view. What I have to do is to point out at least one serious alternative reading to the problematic reading that you raised as an objection to Christianity. And it seems to me that taking an antirealist accommodationist interpretation of divine punishment in natural events is just such a reading, one which should be seriously considered by Christians. So the lesson is that if somebody believes that the traditional view of God punishing entire populations through natural disasters presents a serious obstacle or stumbling block to faith, they should know that there are other alternative ways to think about it that can remove the stumbling block.

Mia: I see, so there is something to be said other than "O man, who art thou that repliest against God?" (Romans 9:20, KJV).

Randal: Hey, I take that warning seriously, for sure. But we must also appreciate that that warning is part of a conversation: being Israel is also reflected in one's willingness to wrestle with the text, and perhaps to end with a different conclusion as a result.

So if you think that's a risk, I'm okay with that. But I will point out that Jesus himself offers teaching that is suggestive of this very different way of thinking about natural disasters. When the Tower of Siloam fell, likely due to an earthquake, it was natural to interpret the event as God's judgment. But Jesus said "Or those eighteen who died when the tower of Siloam fell on them—do you think they were more guilty than all the others living in Jerusalem? I tell you, no!" (Luke 13:4-5a)

And when a man is born blind, the Jews of the day assumed his blindness must be punishment for sin, either his own (in utero, presumably) or that of his parents (John 9:2). But Jesus replied that neither was the case: the man was born blind "so that the works of God might be displayed in him" (v. 3).

So when earthquakes and congenital blindness and other bad natural events occur, we shouldn't immediately assume that they are the result of divine punishment. God may be doing something altogether different. And how tragic it would be if we were to blame people for the suffering they endure through no fault of their own.

If you still think that's a risky position, I'm okay with that.

11

⛵

What if Mary was a child who couldn't consent to bearing a child?

Mia: Okay, enough about natural events. Let's talk about a very *unnatural* one: the virgin birth.

Randal: Virgin birth? Hey, now that's a change of topic! So are you going to raise an objection to this miracle? Or are you going to take issue with the very different nativity stories in Matthew and Luke?

Mia: No, actually I want to focus on the age of Mary and the concept of consent.

Randal: Whoa, that's a new one. I didn't see that coming.

Mia: Well, buckle up, buddy. Things are about to get awkward. So let's start out with your standard children's Christmas pageant. Typically, it will feature, like 12 and 13-year-old kids playing the roles of shepherds, kings, Joseph, and Mary. Cute, right? Especially since we know that the shepherds, kings, and Joseph were not really 12 or 13.

Randal: Yeah, it's always cute seeing kids play adult roles.

Mia: Mary, however, is a different story. While it's common to depict Mary in religious iconography as a young woman in her late teens or perhaps early twenties, in all likelihood she was much younger. The 2006 film *The Nativity Story* is closer to being accurate when it cast then 16-year-old actress Keisha Castle-Hughes as Mary.

Randal: Sixteen? That is awkward.

Mia: It gets worse. It seems that even 16 is likely too old for Mary. The average age of girls at betrothal and marriage in first century Judaism was—wait for it—between 12 and 13. So it seems quite likely that Mary was 12 or 13-years-old at her betrothal to Joseph.[18] In other words, the pubescent kid playing Mary at the Christmas play is spot on as regards her likely age.

Randal: Now this is really getting awkward.

Mia: There is no doubt that current attitudes in the developed West toward child marriage place the contemporary reader at some significant distance from the biblical nativity story. UNICEF defines "child marriage" as a formal or informal matrimonial union that occurs prior to the age of 18. Wikipedia has an interesting article on marriageable ages in history down to today.[19]

Randal: Wikipedia, eh? Going for the top-shelf research, I see.

---

[18] See, for example, Grant R. Osborne, *Matthew, Exegetical Commentary on the New Testament* (Zondervan, 2010), 75.
[19] "Marriageable Age," https://en.wikipedia.org/wiki/Marriageable_age

Mia: Don't be an elitist twit. You can get a lot of good information from Wikipedia and this is a great example. While current practices globally are diverse, on the whole one does find a significant contrast overall between the ancient world and today. In our day the vast majority of countries limit marriage as an independent choice of the individual to 18 or even older. Countries allow child marriage under various conditions such as parental and/or court approval. However, only a tiny minority extend that permission to girls as young as 12 or 13: Trinidad and Tobego allows marriage of females at 12 with parental consent; Iran allows marriage of females at 13 with court approval; Syria also allows child marriage at 13.[20]

Randal: Wow, now that makes me uncomfortable. What are those countries thinking?

Mia: Glad that you share my aversion to this practice. But here's the good news: with these exceptions noted, today, there is a broad consensus that child marriage is suboptimal at best, and an egregious violation of human rights at worse.

Randal: I take your point. But you must concede that at least some of the problems with child marriage are culturally relative. For example, it is possible that in some cultures early marriage provides social goods such as economic security and protection which would not otherwise be available to an unmarried child of that age.

Mia: Fair enough, I'll grant that. But then you must grant that other problems with the practice are intrinsic. For example, it is widely recognized that 12 or 13-year-old girls simply lack the emotional and cognitive maturity that prepares them to enter into a lifelong matrimonial covenant. And the fact that the society in question doesn't recognize the importance of childhood and the gradual nature of cognitive and emotional maturation doesn't change the

---

[20] "Marriageable Age."

fact that these are children who are being robbed of their childhood. The fact that it "could've been worse" doesn't change the reality that it is still very bad.

Randal: 'Robbed' might be a bit strong but for the most part, I agree.

Mia: The picture gets even more complicated when we shift from child marriage to child pregnancy and childbirth. In their article "Adolescent Pregnancy: Where Do We Start?" Linda Bloom and Arlene Escuro outline the multiple physical and emotional complications with teen pregnancy.[21] Needless to say, these complications are exacerbated significantly when the child is a mere 12 or 13-years-old.

So then we face the question: what if Mary was a child who herself couldn't as yet consent to bearing a child?

Randal: I feel the tension here, for sure. It would be a lot easier if I had a good independent reason to believe that Mary was 19 or 20 when she was betrothed to Joseph. And as a parent of a teenage girl, I can say that even 19 or 20 seems terribly young, to say nothing of a 12 or 13-year-old.

But what follows from Mary potentially giving birth as a 13-year-old? It certainly doesn't follow that Christians are obliged to think 12 or 13-year-olds are generally ready for marriage and child-bearing. Rather, what follows is simply that God accommodated to the imperfect cultural mores of the time in which he chose to incarnate his Son. And given the limitations of that context, I have every reason to believe that he would have selected a uniquely mature and pious young lady for the honor.

I think it is also worth pointing out that since God is creator and sustainer of all, he is surely within his rights to act as he sees fit for the redemption of humanity.

---

[21] *Handbook of Nutrition and Pregnancy*, ed. Carol J. Lammi-Keefe, et al (Humana Press, 2008), 101-114.

Mia: Interesting choice of words. You call her a 'young lady'; I call her a *child*. The fact remains that the story of Christ's incarnation is predicated on a child bride giving birth at the very advent of puberty. I find it hard to believe that an omnipotent and perfectly wise God could not have found a better way to bring his son into the world, even if he was accommodating to an imperfect culture.

What is more, it seems to me that this kind of action would naturally suggest to people that God was saying child brides are generally okay, and I think that's a terrible message to give.

Randal: Yeah, I get that. We may have to agree to disagree. But let's also keep in mind that we don't actually *know* Mary's age so this whole discussion is somewhat speculative.

12

⛵

Was Jesus a racist?

Mia: Jesus' origins are not the only point of embarrassment. I also have some concerns about his life.

Randal: His life? Even non-Christians widely laud him as one of the greatest teachers ever.

Mia: Oh, he was definitely an influential teacher, I don't doubt that. But I think you may be looking at him through rose-tinted glasses. If you look at him objectively, you will see that his teaching was something of a mixed bag. Like any other *human being,* he had his bad moments.

Randal: I hope you're not planning to bring up the time he cursed a fig tree (Matthew 21:18-22, Mark 11:12-25). I hear a lot of atheists invoking that one. They read it as nothing more than an embarrassing occasion when Jesus lost his temper and lashed out at a poor, defenseless plant. Understood in this way, this account would be roughly equivalent to a man stubbing his toe on a door and then punching the door in retaliation: not exactly mature behavior.

However, this kind of reading fails to ask, *why* did Matthew and Mark include this story in their gospels? What kind of point were they—and Jesus—aiming to make?

The answer is not hard to find. Jesus' arrival at the fig tree is simultaneous to his arrival at the temple courts. These are the very same temple courts that should've been mediating a way for Jew and Gentile to be reconciled to God. That is, the figurative branches of the temple courts should've been laden with fruit. But instead Jesus finds them empty: all he sees is the corruption of the money lenders and the temple system. And so, the fig tree receives judgement for its barrenness in a performative prophetic act directed at the Temple. The act was *never* about a fig tree: it was *always* about the temple.

Mia: Well, very nice, I can see that you've thought about that. But I wasn't actually going to invoke that case, so it is sort of a moot point.

Randal: Okay, but at the very least that case is a reminder that with Jesus there is far more going on than may initially meet the eye. So we should be careful about hasty judgments concerning his actions.

Mia: Just to be clear, my judgment isn't hasty. I was actually thinking of the Canaanite woman described in Matthew 15:21-28. In that story this poor woman reaches out to Jesus on behalf of her precious child. "Lord, Son of David," she cries, "have mercy on me! My daughter is demon-possessed and suffering terribly."

Imagine the anguish of a mother who is watching her daughter flail about, immobilized, teeth clenched, eyes rolled up in her head. And that mother is helpless, unable to do anything to alleviate her precious child's suffering. So as any desperate mother would, she understandably reaches out to the one man that she believes may be able to help. After all, he has been healing people left and right: surely, he will extend compassion to her too, right?

But after all this, his response is to say *no*, it's not right to use his healing powers on 'dogs'. This desperate woman and her poor suffering daughter, they're *dogs* to him. Not only is that straight-up prejudiced, but it is inexplicably cruel as well.

It's important that we get our minds to grasp how shocking this exchange is. Imagine for a second, a white evangelist in the racially charged south in the 1950s. Let's call him 'Reverend Jackson'. So Reverend Jackson comes to a small town in Alabama to deliver a series of big-tent revival meetings. One evening as he's leaving the meeting, a black woman standing outside calls out to him, "Reverend Jackson, would you please pray for my child? She's very ill." And imagine if Reverend Jackson replied, "It is not right to give the bread for God's white children to the dogs."

Now ask yourself, what would you think of Reverend Jackson if he gave that response? Be honest. Would you think he was an unblemished great and holy revivalist? Or would you think that, whatever his other virtues, he had a cruel racist streak?

Randal: Wow, Mia, you don't make this easy.

Mia: Defending behavior like that shouldn't *be* easy. On the contrary, you should be able to see why it is so shocking. And you should understand why many people don't necessarily find Jesus to be the amazing teacher that you seem to think. He had biases just like the rest of us, although in this case his bias is especially cruel.

Randal: I get your point, but let me respond. I agree that you can take that isolated vignette and describe it in the way you have and it ends up looking pretty bad.

Mia: That's an understatement.

Randal: But I think we need to begin by pulling back a bit to consider some additional factors before we jump to any hasty conclusions.

The first thing I want to point out as I approach this text is that Jesus is consistently on the side of the outsider. He reaches out to the tax collector, the leper, the Samaritan woman, the woman caught in adultery, the overlooked child. Every time there was a person on the margins, he would embrace that individual and he would challenge those who excluded them. And his teaching reinforced his actions such as his parable of the workers in the fields or the banquet which welcomes the outsiders, not to mention his description of the Beatitudes in which the kingdom is reversed. All of this supports his inclusiveness. And in particular, he reached out to and embraced *women*, he taught them, they supported his ministry, they were the first witnesses at the tomb, and they were among the leaders of his movement.

Before you jump to conclusions on a single event, you need to keep this in mind and remember the kind of person we're talking about. Surely if anyone deserves the benefit of the doubt, it's Jesus.

Mia: Okay, so maybe he just had a bad day. How's that?

Randal: Or *maybe* we should revisit what is going on here. The problem with your Reverend Jackson story is you don't give us any backstory. For all we know, the guy has been consistently racist and discriminatory. But what if that wasn't the case? What if Reverend Jackson was actually a leader in the Civil Rights movement? What if he marched alongside Martin Luther King Jr. and supported the bus boycott? In that case, would you just say "Maybe he had a bad day" or would you consider it more likely that he had a different purpose altogether, one that wasn't racist at all?

You have to admit that given a stellar civil rights record, the latter possibility would need to be seriously considered.

Mia: I don't know what you're suggesting that I should seriously consider. What is that "something else" that Jesus might have been doing?

Randal: Look at the story again. How does the Canaanite woman end up looking at the end of the exchange?

Mia: Great, actually. She responds to Jesus with a shrewd comment about how even the dogs receive scraps from the table. And Jesus finally relents and blesses her.

Randal: Exactly, she looks great. But I don't think 'relent' is the right word for Jesus' reaction. Did you ever suppose that maybe Jesus knew how she would respond and he wanted her to reply in a way that would allow her to ennoble herself in this fashion in front of the rabbi and his audience?

The way I see it, Jesus was setting her up to be a hero in her own story.

Mia: That seems a bit too clever by half, doesn't it?

Randal: I don't think so, not at all. Think of a sports trainer who trash talks the athlete he is training—"I don't think you can do it! Prove me wrong!" He's not being mean and he's not actually intending to insult. Instead, he's striving to give the athlete an opportunity to reach the next level of performance. It seems to me that is parallel to what is going on here.

Mia: Maybe, but you're just saying that because you're already a Christian.

Randal: That's partially true: I do come to the teaching of Jesus from a particular perspective because I'm a Christian. But in that case, I'm like a fellow who has worked every day with Reverend Jackson on his revival tour and has already seen his heart for civil rights. From that perspective, *of course* I give him the benefit of the doubt because I know who the man is. So I'm not going to assume he's being racist: rather, I'll take a closer look to see what he really is doing.

It's the exact same with Jesus: if you've already seen his heart for the lost and marginalized and you see how this woman was ennobled in this exchange, I think you have an excellent reason to interpret his actions here not as a *bad day* but rather as an intentional purpose to elevate and ennoble that woman.

Mia: So the idea is, if he's generally a good guy we should assume he's being a good guy here too?

Randal: Call it the benefit of the doubt, if you like. But that makes good sense to me.

What is more, I'm quite sure that there is more going on here. It is also important to heed the immediate context in which this story occurs within the Gospel of Matthew. If we read the first part of Matthew 15 we discover something very interesting. Immediately prior to the exchange with the Canaanite woman we find Jesus having an encounter with the Pharisees and teachers of the law over the issue of ritual washing before a meal. In short, the Jewish leaders complain that Jesus' disciples aren't following this ritual washing and thus that they are thereby violating the traditions of the elders. Jesus responds by charging them with having a greater concern for external purity rather than inner purity. In other words, they have focused on external signs of fidelity to God instead of a transformation of the heart and the fruit of a Spirit-filled life.

Mia: So how does this explain the fact that Jesus called a Canaanite woman a dog?

Randal: Ask yourself two things. First, how do the Pharisees and teachers of the law look at the end of the first exchange? Petty, small-minded, and superficial, right? That's what it looks like if you are concerned with ritual handwashing at the expense of the real works of the Kingdom.

And how does the Canaanite woman look following her encounter? In fact, she's the perfect contrast: although her 'outside' is shameful in the eyes of the religious leaders, she in fact distinguishes herself as a noble, thoughtful, and clever figure.

Isn't this fascinating? After all, Canaanites *were* viewed as equivalent to dogs in Israelite society. And the attitude toward dogs in Israel was *not* a sentimental one. Indeed, they were not far above vermin: unclean, dirty scavengers.

But the biggest tipoff of all is how Jesus appears to be so satisfied that the Canaanite woman gave the right response. You suggested that he 'relented' but that's not right at all. If he was exhibiting a temperamental prejudice, if racism was bubbling up in a moment of weakness, you would expect him to react with defensiveness or irritation to her witty rejoinder: heck, she showed him up!

Instead, he embraces her response as a victory. Like the trainer who was dropping taunts to get his athlete to perform at a higher level, Jesus challenged the woman in this case and stepped back to congratulate her when she rose to the challenge. And that is a stark contrast to the Pharisees and teachers of the law with whom he'd just been sparring.

Mia: I see what you're saying. But what if that woman had *not* responded that way? What if she was instead crushed upon hearing Jesus' words? What if she responded by giving up and walking away in defeat? That could've happened, right? And that risk would seem to be unacceptable just to hope to make this nuanced, sophisticated point.

Randal: If that were a serious risk, it would indeed be a problem. But to return to my analogy, if the trainer knows his athlete well then he isn't risking when he taunts the athlete to encourage her on to higher levels of performance because he knows that she will rise to the challenge.

So could Jesus have had that kind of knowledge of this woman? Could he have known how she would respond? Definitely: time and again, the Gospels describe Jesus as having incisive insight into the hearts, motivations, and character of people. As we read in John 2:25, "he knew what was in each person." For a few other examples see John 4:1, 4:39, 5:6, and 6:61. To consider a couple of specific examples, Jesus knew that Judas would betray him and that Peter would deny him. *He knew people.*

I am reminded of a famous quote from Maya Angelou: "When someone shows you who they are, believe them the first time." I often hear people quoting that in a negative way: as in, don't trust a person who has let you down already. But the quote works both ways. Time and again, Jesus showed us who he is: he cared for the poor, the weak, the marginalized, the forgotten. We need only to believe him. And when we do, we can see that this story is transformed from one of ill-tempered prejudice to a beautiful act of raising up a woman to become the actor in her own story in a way that ennobles her even as it brings healing to her beloved child.

13

Were people really demon-possessed or did they have a natural illness?

Mia: Actually, the story of this poor, demon-possessed daughter leads me straight into another question.

Randal: Which is?

Mia: You've talked a fair bit about God accommodating to understandings of the ancient world. For example, they may have thought of God as manipulating natural events and punishing and blessing people as a result. But you suggested that we can instead recognize that God was, in fact, accommodating to these ancient understandings of the world. We shouldn't just accept that worldview as it is written but rather we should bring it into dialogue with our current understanding and see how it might need to be revised.

Randal: Yeah, I think that's a decent overview of the position I've defended.

Mia: Well okay then, I need to ask: how far does this program of enlightened reinterpretation go? It would appear that ancient people also regularly attributed various psychiatric conditions to malevolent spiritual agents. Like that Canaanite woman with her poor child, for example. She says the child is demon-possessed. But was that really the case? I think that's doubtful. For one thing, descriptions of demon-possession in the Bible look a lot like an epileptic suffering a grand mal seizure.

Countless people have noted the similarity between Gospel accounts of demon possession and an epileptic seizure: with loss of consciousness the patient falls to the ground and goes into a muscularly rigid state, the tonic phase, during which the jaws are clenched and breathing ceases for a few seconds up to half a minute. This is followed by the rhythmic contractions of the muscles in the clonic phase during which the patient may bite his tongue, foam at the mouth, and fling his arms and legs about. During this period he may injure himself, but gradually the jerking movements grow weaker until they finally cease. He may remain unconscious following the seizure for periods of up to half an hour, and upon regaining consciousness he may be fatigued and may sleep for an extended period of time.[22]

With that in mind, consider another case in the Gospels where a man describes the symptoms of his son:

> "Teacher, I brought you my son, who is possessed by a spirit that has robbed him of speech. Whenever it seizes him, it throws him to the ground. He foams at the mouth, gnashes his teeth and becomes rigid. I asked your disciples to drive out the spirit, but they could not." (Mark 9:17-18)

As Robert Stein observes in his Mark commentary, while these are indeed common symptoms of epilepsy, "Mark clearly emphasizes

---

[22] William H. Gaddes, *Learning Disabilities and Brain Function*, (2nd ed., Springer, 1985), 118.

to his readers that the cause of the boy's malady is due to demon possession . . . ."[23]

So I wonder: on your view, were people really demon-possessed or did they just have a natural illness like epilepsy? It seems to me that this all fits perfectly with epilepsy. So why don't you just get rid of the demons and chalk that up to more accommodation?

Randal: That's a fair question. You actually could put it in terms of a *slippery slope*. In short, once you begin on the top of the slope by denying that God really has emotions, or that the sins of Adam and Eve literally changed herbivores into carnivores, or that God literally punishes people through natural disasters, why not keep right on going and do away with the supernatural miracles as well? And if you do in fact do that, then by the end, is there anything of historic Christianity left?

Mia: Yeah, I like that way of putting it. So how *do* you stop the slide?

Randal: Let me tell you a story.

Mia: *Or* you could just answer the question.

Randal: That's *why* I'm telling you the story.

There once was a missionary named Bruce Olson. Mr. Olson became well known in the West for his work with the Motilone people of Colombia. In his book *Bruchko* he describes how he wanted to introduce modern medicine to the tribe but he also didn't want to undermine the witch doctor's authority because he did not believe she was praying to demons, as some Christians have thought. Instead, he believed she was attempting to pray to God and trying to help her people as best she knew how. And he thought it would make a lot of sense if he could enlist her help rather than viewing her as a competitor or enemy.

---

[23] *Mark* (Grand Rapids, MI: Baker Academic, 2008), 433.

Olson accommodated to the witch doctor's understanding in order to win her allegiance. When the tribe contracted pink eye, he persuaded her to use Terramycin, an antibiotic cream, encouraging her to apply the cream while performing her therapeutic chants. And in that way, the tribe recovered because of the cream while the witch doctor retained her status in the community. In this way, Olson won the allegiance of the witch doctor *and* the people.[24] While the witch doctor and her tribal people attributed the healing to the spirits, Olson attributed it to the antibiotic cream. Bottom line: the people *were* healed and that healing came by way of Olson accommodating to the worldview of those being healed.

Later, Olson wanted to help the witch doctor with another outbreak in the tribe that was caused by poor sanitation. To achieve this goal, he simply carried on with his accommodation:

> I went to her and told her that I wanted her to see some of the evil spirits that led to disease and death. I took out my microscope, which I had brought to the jungle, and put a lump of dirt under it. I had her look into the eyepiece.
>
> "Oh, yes, I can see them dancing around," she said and began singing her chants.
>
> Then I put some disinfectant on the dirt and told her to look again. She saw that the disinfectant had killed the germs. It shook her. She had seen that the germs didn't die when she sang her chants.
>
> Over a period of time she introduced disinfectants into the normal ceremonies of the Motilones.[25]

Once again, Olson brought healing and health but he did so in a way that accommodated to the understanding, the worldview, of the people.

---

[24] Bruce Olson, *Bruchko*, 2nd ed. (Seattle: YWAM Publishing, 2005), 129-31.
[25] Olson, *Bruchko*, 132.

Mia: Are you saying that Jesus was actually using scientific methods to deal with natural illnesses the whole while? That these were never *miracles* to begin with?

Randal: No, not quite. I *am* saying that Olson wisely accommodated to the understanding of the Motilones. And it is certainly possible that Jesus did something similar, that he also accommodated to the worldview of his audience. It is possible, for example, that these instances of diagnosed demon possession were, in fact, epileptic seizures.

Mia: So it *was* just natural after all?

Randal: The most important point to remember is that whether the cause of the episode was epilepsy, demon possession, or a combination of the two, the individuals in question *were healed*. And keep in mind as well that healing from epilepsy is not merely like the application of a topical antibiotic cream. Whether the ailment was demons or epilepsy or both, Jesus' healings were the classic examples of miracles, that is, signs of God's action in the world.

Mia: Okay, so you're *not* going to give up on miracles, right?

Randal: No, of course not. Christianity is founded on miracles, above all the miracle of the resurrection of Jesus. Paul said in 1 Corinthians 15:14, the faith stands or falls on the question of whether Jesus rose. So the slippery slope you are proposing is, in fact, a fallacy. The miracles remain as incontrovertible facts: whether Jesus was actually battling with demons or accommodating to an ancient worldview that includes such spiritual beings, the fact is that people *were* healed and those healings were signs of God's action in the world.

Mia: Is this all a round-about way of telling me that you *don't* actually believe in demons?

Randal: Me? No, I do indeed believe that there are malevolent spiritual agencies in the world, beings that we have traditionally called demons.

But I would hasten to add that belief in angels and demons is not a doctrinal issue on the same level as belief in the core matters of the Gospel: triune God, creation, fall, incarnation, atonement, resurrection, and so on. So if a person did have trouble reconciling spiritual agencies with their Christian faith in light of the modern world, I would want to challenge their skepticism but I also wouldn't think that doubt was placing their Christian faith at stake.

14

Why isn't the death of Jesus just one more evil?

Mia: Since we've been talking about miracles, I really want to ask you about the resurrection. But before we get there, perhaps we can talk about the death of Jesus. I've got some big questions about that one.

Randal: Sure, the atoning death of Jesus is at the heart of Christian faith. What do you want to know?

Mia: Simply this: *why isn't the death of Jesus just one more evil?* As I understand it, at the heart of atonement is the idea that Jesus died as our *substitute,* in our place. He took the punishment that was properly owing to us. And this somehow maximizes God's justice. But I think that actually looks positively horrid.

Randal: Horrid? How so?

Mia: Let me give you a real life example. A few years ago, news broke of the case of Juan Silva Sr. who was arrested for a fatal hit-and-run in 2013 after he turned himself in to police. Silva was convicted and sent to jail. But it turns out that he issued a false plea in order to protect his 22-year-old son who was, in fact, the perpetrator of the crime.[26]

Some people may admire Silva for his commitment to his son while others will be offended by his subversive attempt to deceive the court. But everyone is in agreement that justice is not served when a father willingly goes to prison for his son's crime. An act like this does not serve the cause of justice. The reason is simple: each individual must be held guilty for the crime he committed. Guilt cannot be transferred from one party to another. As the saying goes, if the son did the crime, then the son should do the time.

Randal: That's an interesting case, but there is an obvious *disanalogy* between Silva's action and the atonement: in your scenario, the father and son were attempting to *deceive* the court. And the son, in particular, was attempting to get away with an illegal action. By contrast, there certainly is no deception in the atonement.

Mia: That misses the point: the reason they resorted to deception is precisely because *no court would ever accept what is clearly an unjust arrangement.* If the father goes to court for his son, it doesn't address the cause of justice at all. Rather, it is but *one more miscarriage of justice:* not only does a guilty party walk scot-free but an innocent party is punished for the crime, thereby multiplying the injustice. And that's just wrong.

So back to my simple question: how does the atonement redeem anybody? Why isn't it instead just one more injustice? The guilty party walks scot-free while an innocent party is punished on their behalf.

---

[26] See Samira Puskar, Jon Schuppe, and Bob Vasilopulos, "Juan G. Silva, Dad, Who Took Rap for Son's Hit-and-Run, To Leave Prison," (July 27, 2015), *NBC News*, https://www.nbcnews.com/news/us-news/dad-who-took-rap-sons-hit-run-leave-prison-report-n398956

Randal: Yup, it's like the old story of the whipping boy. According to the story, a child in medieval Europe would supposedly be designated to be beaten whenever the royal prince would misbehave: since it would be dishonoring for the prince to be beaten, the guilt was instead transferred to the whipping boy under the logic that *somebody* had to be punished. But of course, that 'logic' doesn't satisfy justice: it just adds one more injustice.

Mia: Were whipping boys really a thing?

Randal: Eh, I'm not so sure. Historians are skeptical about that. But either way, the story certainly conveys the idea that you're chaffing against.

Mia: Yeah, well I didn't really *need* another example, but neither will I refuse it. And you're right: whipping some poor boy for the sins of the prince would definitely look to me like just one more offense.
So how do *you* explain the logic of atonement?

Randal: I think the first thing I want to say is that I believe the heart of your objection is not against the Christian doctrine of atonement *per se* but rather against a specific *theory* of atonement, namely the penal substitutionary theory. According to that theory, Christ reconciles us to the Father by being punished in our place and having our sin transferred to him. But many Christians do not accept that theory. One can reject penal substitution *theory* of atonement while retaining the core *doctrine* of atonement.

Mia: So what is the *right* theory then?

Randal: In fact, there are many theories of atonement: ransom, Christus victor, exemplar, Girardean, governmental, recapitulation, and others. Each aims to offer an overarching framework to interpret how God actually works to reconcile us in Christ. But I don't actually endorse any one of them.

The key, from my view, is to note that the church on the whole has never committed to insisting that any one of these theories is *the* correct one. So while the church teaches the atoning work of Christ—indeed, that teaching is at the heart of her proclamation—it has never formally dictated a specific theory of how that work should be understood.

That's one reason why I don't hold to a specific theory. Rather, I think that the New Testament provides a rich multiplicity of word pictures or metaphors and that each one of them offers a particular insight even if none of them can sustain an overarching theory.

Mia: But how can you expect people to buy into the atonement if you don't know how it works?

Randal: That's like asking "How can I benefit from this medicine if I don't understand how it works?" Not only may a patient benefit from a treatment that they don't understand but scientists may actually identify and apply an effective new treatment without knowing precisely how or why it works. If that's true in the case of science and medicine, I certainly think it can also be true in the case of theology.

Mia: I dunno, I think that you're skirting the main issue. Surely you can say something more about how the atonement functions than that?

Randal: Absolutely, there are many rich and compelling theoretical accounts that one might consider. But rather than seek understanding through *theory*, for this conversation I think we're better off seeking understanding through *story*. The heart of atonement, as you correctly observed, is the idea of substitution: Christ does indeed stand in our place, accomplishing what we could not, and thereby reconciling us to the Father. And there are endless images of the redemptive substitute to which one can appeal for inspiring analogues.

One of my favorites is in the wonderful 1998 animated film *The Iron Giant*. In the film, a giant robot from outer space comes to earth and befriends a lonely young boy named Hogarth. The film is set in 1957 at the height of the 'Red Scare' following the Soviet Union launch of Sputnik into space. As the town begins to catch glimpses of the Iron Giant, people start to talk and the suspicion arises that the Soviets are planning to attack the United States. This leads to the military marshalling forces. Then through a series of unfortunate events a nuclear warhead is fired at the town. As the warhead roars toward the bucolic setting, the Iron Giant rockets up into the sky and meets it head-on: the Maine coast is lit up by a nuclear fireball in the heavens as people witness in shock that the Iron Giant—the very individual that people had feared—gives his life for them and thereby provides the very means of their redemption.

That is one story, but there are countless others that tell a similar tale of one individual stepping forth into the mess of history and saving people from themselves by giving him or herself in their place, absorbing the destructive impact of their choices and thereby offering the way to redemption.

No one story can capture all that the Christian doctrine of atonement is proposing, but I think that stories are often more successful at enabling us to recognize the deep grain of atonement, grace, and salvation than technical theories.

Oh, and one more thing: *The Iron Giant* does not end with the death of our hero. Instead, it ends with, well, you should probably just watch it . . .

15

Isn't a natural explanation more plausible than the resurrection?

Mia: So you're not going to tell me how *The Iron Giant* ends? Bummer. But I'm guessing there probably is a resurrection at the end. And that's actually the next thing I'd like to talk about: the resurrection of Jesus.

Randal: Good, because belief in Jesus' resurrection is not only a matter of faith. There is some surprisingly strong historical evidence for the miraculous resurrection.

Mia: Too bad the reader can't see my raised eyebrow.

Randal: Yeah, or my eye-roll in response to your raised eyebrow.

Skeptics often make a couple of critical mistakes in their dismissal of the resurrection. First, they assume that the New Testament is a single document. In fact, it is a complex library of writings from the first century and several of those writings provide important historical witnesses to the resurrection.

Second, they often are skeptical of these writings just because they are included in the Bible. But before these texts were ever recognized as being part of a religious collection of 'inspired' writings, they were works of secular history—everyday letters and biographies—which tell something amazing about how this extraordinary person Jesus impacted others.

Of all the documentation that we find recorded in the New Testament, I am particularly intrigued by the evidence of 1 Corinthians 15:3-8. That text captures the essence of the Gospel proclamation: the death of Jesus for our sins, his resurrection, and his post-resurrection appearances to Peter, James, 500 others, and last of all to Paul himself.

While Paul quotes that passage in his letter to Corinth from about AD 54, he notes that he relayed that information to the Corinthians on his earlier visit in 51. What is more, he also says that he had received it earlier still. So when did *Paul* receive this teaching? Well, in Galatians 1 Paul includes some invaluable details about his own conversion. Scholars believe that Paul likely had his famous Damascus Road experience, that event which changed him from the chief persecutor of the disciples to being himself a disciple, in about the year 34, approximately a year after the death of Jesus. And as I said, in Galatians 1:18-19, Paul then recounts that three years after this he went up to Jerusalem and met for a couple of weeks with Cephas, that is Peter, as well as James, the brother of Jesus.

So the very latest that Paul would've received this teaching is in the year 37 from Peter and James. And of course, they didn't formulate this teaching just for Paul. By this time, it would already have been a fixture of the teaching of the early church.

Note a couple of things here. First, that means that we have evidence that the core confession about Jesus' meritorious death and resurrection was already circulating in the early Christian community *in Jerusalem* and within *a couple of years of the death of*

Jesus. There's no room for legend here. We are within a couple of years of the events. And we need an explanation to account for the origin of belief in the resurrection, by implication a tomb that was found empty, and the claim of these early disciples that they saw Jesus raised again.

Mia: Look, you've obviously thought about this carefully and you have all your nice little apologetic ducks in a row. But before you say anything else, I'd like to talk for a moment about another miracle worker from ancient history . . . Apollonius of Tyana.

Randal: *Apollonius of Tyana?!* Oh come on, there's no comparison between Jesus and that footnote of ancient history.

Mia: Wait, *no* comparison? That would seem to be a bit of an overstatement. This is what Bart Ehrman wrote of him:

> Even before he was born, it was known that he would be someone special. A supernatural being informed his mother that the child she was to conceive would not be a mere mortal but would be divine. He was born miraculously, and he became an unusually precocious young man. As an adult he left home and . . .[27]

Randal: Look, I'm going to stop you right there. I'm familiar with that passage from Ehrman. He's trying to draw a comparison between Apollonius and Jesus but it is deeply misleading. There just isn't the same historical evidence to ground the claims about Apollonius.

Mia: He lived in the first century just like Jesus.

Randal: But the evidence we have of his life comes from a *single source*—the writer Philostratus—and that dates to the early *third*

---

[27] *Did Jesus Exist? The Historical Argument for Jesus of Nazareth* (New York: HarperOne, 2012), 208.

century. By contrast, the Christians have a library of witnesses for Jesus dating to within decades—and in the case of the creedal formula in 1 Corinthians 15:3-7, perhaps a *couple of years*—of the life of the man. If Apollonius is the best parallel the skeptic has to offer, it shows how strong the evidence for Jesus really is.

So thanks for that, I guess!

Mia: Sorry, I didn't realize that the Ehrman quote would be such a trigger for you! I think you like him even less than Carl Satan, oops, I meant 'Sagan'.

But hey, my point isn't really about Apollonius of Tyana, anyways.

Randal: Then why did you bring him up?

Mia: I'm making a more general point. Consider an analogy. Two men are accused of a crime. One is poor and the other is rich and each needs to put on a defense. The poor bloke can't afford a lawyer of his own and so he gets the overworked public defender. By contrast, the rich guy gets a team of world class lawyers and they enlist another team of researchers and assistants to scour around for all the possible evidence to develop a range of viable theories all of which can raise reasonable doubt in the minds of a jury.

Even if the evidence implicating each man is similar, we can all guess which one will get a better defense and thus which is more likely to be found not guilty. If you look for enough evidence and you have enough capable lawyers on your team, you can get away with almost anything.

Randal: And your point is . . . ?

Mia: I recognize that there is *some* evidence for Jesus, sure. But there is also *some* evidence for Apollonius. In terms of their subsequent defenses, you've got to admit that poor Apollonius is at something of a disadvantage here. After all, Jesus has had countless scholars working on his case for the last two thousand years. By contrast,

Apollonius has had almost none. So you've got to ask: how might the tables have turned if it was Apollonius rather than Jesus who had a team of scholars over two millennia seeking to amass a case for *his* miracles?

Randal: So your point is that we ought to recognize more miracle workers than just Jesus?

Mia: No, quite the opposite. My point is that if you work long and hard enough, you'll eventually come up with something to favor your client. But setting that dogged advocacy aside I have to ask: isn't a natural explanation far more plausible than the resurrection?

Randal: I appreciate your statement for one key reason: I think you accurately describe the kind of dismissive thinking that burbles just under the surface from many so-called skeptics.

But I think there is also a huge hole at the center of your response. Somewhat tongue-in-cheek, you lament the fact that Apollonius was largely forgotten while Jesus had a unique historical impact. But you never explore the reasons for that difference. Why was it *Jesus* that had a uniquely massive impact on world history while Apollonius has been relegated to a mere footnote? Why did Jesus attract all the defenders?

See, I would suggest that your illustration has things quite wrong. It isn't so much that people believe Jesus supernaturally rose from the dead because he had a team of advocates scouring the historical record for any scintilla of evidence to sustain that belief. More to the point, those advocates are not merely hired guns being paid to come up with any evidence to vindicate their client. Rather, these are faithful believers who have themselves been impacted by the uniquely powerful evidence for this man. If you want to understand why Jesus amassed such a formidable team of supporters, just look at the evidence. And if you are willing to consider that evidence with an open mind, you might well find it compelling for the same reasons.

Mia: I *have* an open mind. But that doesn't mean it is open to just any incredible claim. If a guy you know and respect suddenly told you that he was abducted by aliens and teleported to a distant planet would you consider the truth of his claim? Or would you remain committed to seeking a natural explanation?

We have overwhelming evidence that dead people don't rise, and even if I can't explain exactly what happened two thousand years ago, that doesn't mean that resurrection moves to the head of the live options.

Randal: I think you raise a good general point here. Many people have a background plausibility framework—that is, a set of assumptions about the way the world is—which lead them to be highly skeptical of resurrection claims, to such a degree that they may simply be closed to the possibility for practical purposes. Others are far more open.

To take your alien example, obviously if I already believe that aliens exist and that they've possibly visited earth and if you are persuaded that aliens definitely *don't* exist, we will both approach the testimony of that guy differently. I'll be more open to considering his claims than you would be. Neither one of us is wrong.

But there is also a danger here, namely the danger that one will screen out legitimate evidence *a priori* just because it doesn't fit one's assumptions about the world. I think, at this point of the Ptolemaic astronomers of the Middle Ages. According to their view, the heavens were eternal and unchanging and were defined by crystalline spheres in which heavenly objects—sun, moon, and stars—were embedded. This worldview didn't allow for things such as comets (which definitely didn't respect the spheres since their oblong orbits cut right through them) and supernovae (in which massive stars would suddenly explode).

Interestingly, as historian of science Thomas Kuhn pointed out, many of these astronomers would diligently record celestial events that fit with their assumptions. But they would simply *ignore* any evidence for events that didn't fit their paradigm such as the seemingly random appearance of comets and supernovae. So, for example, a supernova that appeared brightly in the night sky and was recorded dutifully by Chinese astronomers was simply ignored by their European counterparts The lesson is that we all need to be careful not to allow our prior assumptions about the world to restrict the evidence we are willing to consider.

So when it comes to your observation that dead people don't rise, yeah, obviously that is generally the case. But is it possible that it *could* happen? Well, I just ask that you keep an open mind and look at the historical evidence.

Mia: And what if I do look at the evidence and I'm not persuaded? What if I'm happier saying that there must be a natural explanation rather than your supernatural miracle?

Randal: I'd say a couple of things. First, I find that skeptics often approach the question with a troubling lack of nuance. It's like they have an on/off switch: either the evidence is sufficient to persuade them that something extraordinary did, indeed, happen, or they can just dismiss it outright. However, there is a whole lot of space in between those two positions. For example, you could say "I'm not sure what to think about this, and the evidence leaves me a little less persuaded in the truth of my position than I was before. But it isn't enough to get me to change my mind, as yet." I can respect that position. What I can't respect is if you simply wave your hand and say "Nah, the world couldn't be like that."

And that leads me to my second point: while you may conclude that the evidence isn't enough to persuade you, I'd hope you could at least recognize that you don't, as yet, have a satisfactory natural explanation for this evidence and thus that you should keep working on one. I recognize that worldviews are rarely changed with a single inexplicable historical event. But a single inexplicable historical event can be the first step toward changing your worldview

16

Why does God torture people in hell?

Mia: I have no doubt that we could spend several hours going back and forth on the resurrection, but the show must go on. I think next we should talk about the afterlife. I've got a *lot* of questions here. Like, for starters, why does God torture people in hell? What kind of loving, merciful God is that?

Randal: Alright, that's a big topic, but perhaps I can head off some of your skepticism at the pass. Hell is a difficult doctrine, no doubt. But it is also rendered *more* difficult by particular understandings of the fate of the damned, understandings that I and many other Christians do not accept. In particular, I *reject* the view of hell as a sort of divine torture chamber in which God pours out his wrath on poor, damnable wretches for eternity.

Far more plausible is the view of hell as being like a self-chosen exile. As Timothy Keller puts it, "hell is simply one's freely chosen identity apart from God on a trajectory into infinity."[28]

---

[28] *The Reason for God: Belief in an Age of Skepticism* (Penguin, 2008), 80.

Mia: That sounds like wishful thinking. You're just trying to make hell fit into your own modern and appropriately soft views of justice. But hell is the ultimate square peg to try to fit in your round hole of modern enlightened thinking.

Randal: I don't think so. There's actually a lot of evidence to support a view of hell as a self-imposed exile. We could start with the fact that Jesus warns on several occasion of hell as weeping and gnashing of teeth: for example, in Matthew 13:42 and Luke 13:28.

Mia: How does that help? That sounds *exactly* like God tossing people into a dungeon.

Randal: Look closer. It is true that the image of weeping expresses regret and anguish. But the image of gnashing in the Greek conveys rage, like a dog bearing its teeth in an act of aggression. For another example, look at how the Jewish leaders gnashed their teeth in rage right before they stoned Stephen to death in Acts 7:54.

So the message of this image is that some people will hate God and continue in their act of rebellion in, as Keller said, that freely chosen identity apart from God into eternity.

Mia: I still don't see how that improves things.

Randal: How does it not? God gives us over to our own free wills. God isn't a cruel, vindictive judge. Instead, he grants us the dignity to choose our own fate.

Mia: I think you're engaging in some selective reading. In the New Testament hell is also depicted with unimaginably horrifying images like a lake of fire and a roaring furnace. And passages like Revelation 14:9-11 and 20:10 and 15 suggest that *God* is the one who tosses people into this terrible place. Awful stuff!

And even if I granted your convenient renovation of hell, it still is a fundamentally offensive and unmerciful image. You suggest it is noble to allow people to inflict misery on themselves. But is it really so noble to allow people to continue on a perpetual cycle of self-imposed misery and despair, just because they *choose* it? That's far from obvious.

Imagine that Jones comes to revile his own life so much that he begins to mutilate himself, cutting and burning his own flesh even as he screams and curses in agony. "Stop Jones!" you plead, but he continues on undeterred with even greater intensity. At what point would you intervene in the situation by physically restraining Jones so that he could no longer carry out his tormented, all-consuming, self-loathing torture?

The situation of Jones in that scenario is very much like the situation in which Jones is cut off from God eternally in self-imposed isolation. Only in the latter case, Jones' suffering is unimaginably worse. You want me to accept that God is going to stand passively by while Jones forever engages in tormented spiritual self-mutilation? Why would God allow this to occur? Why wouldn't he intervene? Why wouldn't he restrain the poor wretch?

Randal: You've definitely painted a bleak and emotionally compelling picture. But keep in mind as C.S. Lewis said, that the joy of the universe cannot be held hostage by the fact that some people end up being implacable rebels.[29]

Mia: No way man, I'm not letting you off with that. I am reminded here of the documentary *Solitary Nation* that was featured on the PBS program Frontline. When you think about it, the idea of hell that you're trying to sell is very much like the depiction of those prisoners left to rot in their cells. The film focuses on several months in the solitary confinement unit of the Maine State Prison. The unit consists of several small cell rooms with heavy doors and Plexiglas windows where violent offenders are locked up for 23 hours per day.

---

[29] *The Great Divorce* (New York: HarperOne, 2001), 137.

Many start off facing the weeks or months they must spend in solitary with a stoic optimism. But soon they are in a free fall spiral of decay. With nothing to do and no hope, they plug their toilets to flood the unit, they slide feces under the doors and wipe it on windows, and they gash their wrists with tiny razors, slathering themselves with pulses of deep red blood. The message that comes through is that solitary confinement has a way of shattering one's psychological wellness and drawing the prisoner ever further into a spiral of misery and despair.

Randal: Yeah, believe me, I remember.

Mia: One furious prisoner had taken to threatening to kill the warden and guards if he isn't allowed back into the general prison population so that he may again have visits with his wife and two daughters. As he makes his matter-of-fact plea to the warden—in effect "Get me out of here or I'll kill you"—it sounds a lot like this idea of hell as consisting of self-imposed exile.

That is unspeakably cruel and barbaric, and yet, your 'enlightened' view of hell sounds a lot like Maine State's solitary confinement unit: lock people up indefinitely and leave them to cut themselves, beat the walls, flood their cells, and smear feces on the tiny windows. Now maybe that is an improvement over a divinely run torture chamber, but if so, the improvement is nominal at best. It still is an endlessly cruel way to treat human beings. It's bad enough when it unfolds over a course of weeks or months. But in your vision of hell, it unfolds over an *eternity*. I don't have *words* for how awful and cruel that sounds.

Randal: Much depends on the metaphor or analogy we choose to think about hell. In *The Great Divorce* C.S. Lewis describes this self-imposed exile as like an endlessly dreary life in a rainy British city.

Mia: Right, but how is that not simply a bald attempt to make you *feel better?* It seems to me that the horror of the solitary confinement unit in a prison is a far more apt comparison, especially when you digest the full horror of the warnings about hell that one finds throughout Jesus' teaching. I just don't see much advantage here.

Randal: Okay, I'll say this. The solitary confinement image is an awful one, I agree. And viewed from that perspective, the advantage of conceiving hell as self-imposed isolation is limited.

This is probably a good point for me to say that I don't hold to the view of hell as eternal conscious torment, even of this self-imposed sort. I believe, rather, that hell involves a resurrection to judgment. And that judgment will result, ultimately, in the destruction of the individual and the cessation of their existence (Matthew 10:28). So on my view, hell isn't a matter of God torturing people or allowing them to torture themselves for eternity. Rather, God resurrects people and then turns them over to their self-destructive impulses resulting in their own spiral that culminates in their ceasing to exist.

17

⛵

Why would God resurrect people
only to kill them again?

Mia: Wait, so you believe God resurrects people so that he can subject them to a final judgment which culminates in them ceasing to exist?

Randal: Yes, the view is called annihilationism and it has been defended by Christians back to the early church and throughout church history. And it is consistent with evangelical Christian conviction.

Mia: Slow down and don't be so defensive, man. So let me get this straight: you said that on your view God resurrects people to judgment?

Randal: Yes, we read of that in Daniel 12:2. And Jesus reaffirms the teaching in John 5:25 and 28-9.

Mia: Uh huh. So let's be clear: evil people die. They go into the ground. Their bodies rot to nothing. They've returned to their resting place in the earth. Finally, all is well with the world.

And then God goes through the trouble of resurrecting these evil sinners, reconstituting their bodies like you read in Ezekiel 37, bringing back together dried bones, reattaching ligaments and muscles, replacing the organs and covering it all in flesh, and finally breathing in the breath of life. And he does all that just so Jesus can cut them down again with a sanctified AR-15?

Come on, what's the point of that?

Randal: You're really up with the provocative images. But I think this is all wrong. You're trying to poison the well with your image. First of all, it doesn't take God any effort at all to resurrect a creature. It's not like it's *difficult*, as if it requires an investment of time and effort. He is omnipotent, remember.

Mia: Fine, but why *does* he do it?

Randal: Fair question. Well, here's my answer: it's a matter of justice. Let me give you an illustration, one that is more accurate than yours.

Mia: Go for it.

Randal: So imagine that Jones commits mass murder and he is now in jail, his appeals exhausted, facing an imminent execution for his crimes. There is a prison riot and as the melee ensues, Jones is critically injured. By the time the paramedics get to him he is about to die. Would it be right for them to allow him to die in that moment if they can save his life?

Mia: Seems simpler, no? He's going to be killed soon anyway.

Randal: The issue isn't what is simpler. The issue is what action is right and sometimes the right thing to do is not the simplest.

The paramedics' job is to stabilize injured prisoners and get them to the hospital and the job of the medical doctors is to get the patients to recover. They all faithfully carry out their specific mandates. And they do so even though they know that Jones is on death row waiting to be executed for his crimes. They do it because justice requires that they fulfill their mandates so that Jones dies not as a result of incidental injuries sustained in a prison riot but rather as a result of state-inflicted punishment.

Mia: Okay, so what?

Randal: When a person dies they are not dying as punishment for their sins. They are dying because they are mortal and they simply succumbed to that mortality due to the incidental circumstances of their life. But that death wasn't itself a *punishment* for their rejection of God.

And so it would not be proper for God to allow that to be the end of the story any more than it is proper to allow Jones to die of injuries sustained in a prison riot rather than as a result of official state-inflicted punishment.

Mia: Then why doesn't God just kill people by way of annihilation for their wicked rejection of him when they are already dying in their mortal bodies? Kill two birds with one stone, as it were. Why does he go to the trouble of a future resurrection that repeats and thereby extends the process? It seems wholly gratuitous.

Randal: I think we have to be somewhat cautious here since we don't understand much about the future resurrection but we can say that it will manifest God's justice and perfect nature.

Mia: I'm still at a loss as to why that cannot happen simultaneously with death. Why does God need to go through a resurrection?

Randal: For example, it is possible that there is particular significance about a single event of judgment in which God finally sets the world aright, one that reveals his perfect and just nature to all creatures. But to sum up, I would simply say that if annihilation is not simultaneous with death, as I believe, then it follows that God has good and morally sufficient reasons to bring about a general resurrection to judgment after death. And I'm content to leave it there.

Mia: Well, I'm not content that you left it there.

18

How can it be just to damn minors?

Mia: There are many other problems with the Christian theology of damnation. Heck, I could go on all day.

Randal: Well, I don't know if we have *all* day. But what's your next big one?

Mia: I've got a serious problem with the damnation of children.

Randal: Wait, who said anything about the damnation of children? Many Christians believe that children are accepted into God's kingdom if they die before they reach the age of accountability.

Mia: Many? But not all?

Randal: It is true that some Christians defend the view that small children or even infants who die may be damned or lost forever. But I certainly don't hold that view and I'm quite sure it is very much in the minority.

Mia: You're 'sure' it's "very much in the minority"? I'm inclined to say the fact that *any* Christians would believe that an infant could end up in hell before she can even learn her own name is appalling.

Randal: I agree; it's not my view. Like I said, I believe that most Christians would adhere to some sort of age of accountability.

Mia: Right, and when is that, exactly?

Randal: My daughter is now an adult, but I can't help but personalize the question. See, I wrestled with this when she was growing up. Was she damnable as a child? Could she have been culpably separated from God for eternity when she was but four-years-old? And if so, what about when she was three-years-old? Or three-months-old? What is the point of damnability such that once a child crosses it that child will be damned if she has, as yet, failed to believe or do the right things?

Mia: I'm glad you didn't simply treat these problems as mere academic conundrums. From my perspective, it would be unimaginable to think that the God who is Love, and the Jesus who described entry to his Kingdom as becoming like a little child, would damn a four-year-old to hell.

Randal: Yes, I agree. If I were to push beyond that intuition in search of an underlying reason for my confidence, I'd say that the four-year-old had not yet reached that age of accountability, that is, the age at which point a person becomes accountable for their beliefs and actions (or perhaps entrenched in implacable patterns of rebellion). Of course, this is not to suggest that a four-year-old is completely unaccountable for their beliefs and actions. Rather, it is just to say that a four-year-old is not ultimately accountable for a decision so momentous that it could result in their eternal damnation.

Mia: Be thankful for small mercies, I guess. You know, there is a reason that civilized nations do not subject children to adult prison sentences. First of all, their prefrontal cortex is undeveloped. This is the last part of the brain to reach maturity, and it affects a broad range of cognitive abilities including, among others, the ability of young people to anticipate the consequences of one's behavior. This is why, for example, teenagers are much more likely to engage in high risk behavior than are adults. If you don't believe me, just take a few minutes to peruse the range of idiotic teen stunts memorialized on YouTube.

Randal: That's okay. I don't need YouTube's help: I just need to remember back to my high school days. Yikes.

Mia: Exactly. Consider a legal mandate that says all children who talk back to their parents are to be stoned. But a twenty-year-old can anticipate more fully the consequences of their actions than a fifteen-year-old can. And a fifteen-year-old can anticipate them more fully than a five or ten-year-old can. Given this fact, we recognize that it is wrong to apply to minors the same punishments as one extends to adults, because their prefrontal cortex is not sufficiently developed to anticipate to the same degree the consequences of their actions.

And there's a second major issue as well: hormonal changes. According to the American Academy of Child and Adolescent Psychiatry (AACAP), the advent of puberty brings with it a range of emotional and behavioral issues in teenagers which are considered part of normal teenage development. These include changing one's appearance, withdrawing from various aspects of family life, increased argumentativeness with authority figures, and emotional ups and downs. These are the reasons why civilized nations do not levy capital punishment on legal minors.

But you're saying Christianity would say otherwise?

Randal: It depends on the Christian.

This is a serious problem, I agree. One of the difficulties is that culpability seems to come in degrees but salvation/damnation is a binary thing: either you're saved or you aren't. And if you aren't, then you get capital punishment by definition.

I will say this. In Romans 2:12 Paul suggests that one's guilt or culpability is relative to the background knowledge of each individual. Jesus makes a similar point in Luke 12:47-48. And this I do know: however it works out, I don't have a doubt at all that God judges in a far more merciful and wise fashion than I ever could.

19

⛵

If your children could end up damned forever, shouldn't you be an antinatalist?

Mia: I don't think we're quite done with the damnation of children yet.

Randal: What more do you want to say?

Mia: I believe the implications of hell are much more radical than you probably recognize and I'd like to explore that further.

Let's start here: Christians believe that Christianity is pro-children, right?

Randal: Yeah, definitely.

Mia: Children are a blessing from the Lord and God blessed Adam and Eve and gave them kids. So all things being equal, Christians should want to have children.

Randal: Yes, I agree with that as well. I don't think that God's words in Genesis 1:28 are a command to have children so much as they are a *blessing* that we may have children (cf. Psalm 127:3). So what's the problem?

Mia: I think you need to digest your views on damnation and reconcile them with your views on children. Antinatalism is the philosophical view that the birth of new human beings is, in some sense, a disvalue and should be avoided. To be sure, antinatalists disagree widely on their *reasons* for assigning a disvalue to the creation of new human life. One person might be an antinatalist because of the anticipated quality of life of the newborn—"I couldn't bring a new life into a world with all this suffering"—while another person might be an antinatalist because of the impact of yet another human life on planet earth— "The planet has exceeded its carrying capacity for human beings!"

Randal: Antinatalism is very far from the Christian perspective of children as a blessing. So I don't see what your point is.

Mia: Don't speak too fast. You've said that you reject the view of hell as eternal conscious torment, whether divinely imposed or self-imposed, right?

Randal: Correct.

Mia: But you *could* also be wrong, correct? I mean, you may think you have decent arguments for your view but they are not foolproof.

Randal: Sure, we see through a glass darkly, as Paul said, so I could definitely be wrong in my beliefs: I'm just a fallible human being.

Mia: Right, so on your view you are very possibly wrong and maybe there *is* this terrible eternal hell after all. So how bad might that hell be?

Randal: Worse than we can imagine.

Mia: 'Worse than we can imagine'? I hope you don't mind if I at least give it a try. One of the worst diseases I've read about is Stevens-Johnson syndrome. In this terrible condition, your body is covered with welts and open sores that look like third-degree burns and you're gripped by mind-numbing pain. Even the lightest touch can slough your skin off in bloody hunks, leaving the patient to writhe in unimaginable agony. This awful condition can even create blisters inside the mouth and on the eyelids. It doesn't get worse than that.

And yet, if we take the biblical authors seriously, this fate is *nothing* compared to the suffering of the damned.

You've offered a far more humane vision of hell than some other views on offer, but you could be wrong and another far less humane view could be the right one. And yet, that possibility alone should be enough to undermine your willingness to subject children to that enormous risk. I'll put it like this:

11. The belief that there is a significant chance that any future child you might have would be born with a horrifying and untreatable disease like Stevens-Johnson syndrome would provide a good reason to avoid having children.
12. Hell is unimaginably worse than Stevens-Johnson syndrome.
13. If the belief that there is a significant chance that any future child you might have would be born with Stevens-Johnson syndrome would provide a good reason to avoid having children, then the belief that there is a significant chance that any future child you might have would ultimately experience eternal conscious torment provides a maximally powerful reason to avoid having children.
14. There is a significant chance that any future child you might have would ultimately experience eternal conscious torment.
15. Therefore, you have a maximally powerful reason to avoid having children.

Ergo, if you believe in hell, you should be an antinatalist: you shouldn't have children.

Randal: That's an interesting way to look at it. But no surprise, I am not an antinatalist.

Mia: But why? Isn't it irresponsible, reckless even, for you to assume that kind of risk?

Randal: No, I think there are several factors to consider that override your concern. First of all, children are indeed a blessing and we should think of them as such.

As for the risk that I could be wrong about hell, we should recognize that all life is an assumption of risk. *You* could be wrong about hell, too. Moreover, any person—whether Christian or atheist or anything else—assumes an unknown risk about the range of illnesses their future child may endure, let alone all the other types of suffering that is possible. But if we always refused to act based upon possible risk, we would be immobilized. At some point, we have no choice but to act.

Mia: But the stakes are unimaginably greater in *this* case. We're not just talking about a cancer diagnosis or trial of spousal abuse, as terrible as those experiences might be. We're talking about the risk that this individual's entire life may be a mere momentary flash prior to uncountable eons of unimaginable torment.

From that perspective, what could possibly override *that* risk?

Randal: I think you should consider the fact that your argument applies to everyone, not just people who believe in hell. Do *you* have some powerful argument to demonstrate that that terrible scenario you describe is not even possibly true? And if you don't, doesn't it follow that *you* shouldn't have children?

Mia: I don't have to worry about that since I'm just a voice in your head.

Randal: Touché, but that doesn't mean you can ignore the consequences of your own position. If you want to argue that a Christian shouldn't have children based on the mere possibility of this scenario's being true, then *nobody* should have children based on the mere possibility of this scenario's being true. In other words, if your scenario proves anything it proves that we should *all* be antinatalists. And at that point, you no longer have a specific objection to Christianity in particular: in short, you proved *too much*.

Mia: Fair enough, maybe we all *should* be antinatalists. I'm perfectly fine with that, but it is still bad news for your religion.

20

If Christianity is true, shouldn't Christians show more evidence of sanctification?

Mia: It's often been said that the biggest objection to Christianity is the life of Christians.

Randal: There's more truth in that statement than I'd like to admit. One of the difficult if not outright painful aspects of Christianity is the fact that Christians can be awful, awful to one another and awful to other people.

This fact really came home for me when I started teaching church history to seminarians in the fall of 2003.

Mia: I feel for ya: teaching can be painful!

Randal: That's not what I meant. I love teaching! But I've taught church history for 17 years now and the sober truth is that I've seen many students get their faith rattled by seeing just how messy church history can be.

Mia: Yeah? Well, I'm not surprised. Okay, what's the *worst* thing you've ever seen someone do in the name of Christ?

Randal: The *worst* thing? Ugh, okay, you asked for it. I don't really know about *the* worst but I can think of plenty of perfectly terrible examples. One of the cases that immediately comes to mind is recorded in Foxe's *Book of Martyrs*. This work is a famous martyrology, a bloody volume of Reformation-era anti-Papist Protestant polemic which chronicles all the horrors one can imagine.

In a chapter titled "The Guernsey Martyrs," we read about three women who were subjected to horrific suffering at the hands of some zealous Catholics, and all for their Protestant faith.[30] They were all hanged on a gallows and while two had the relative mercy of being strangled as a result, in the case of the third, the rope broke and she tumbled into the fire that had been kindled below.

Mia: What?! So they tried to hang a poor woman just for the 'sin' of being Protestant and she was strangled *and* burned alive?

Randal: Incredibly, it gets worse. The lady was at a late stage of pregnancy and her belly ripped open when she fell into the flames. The infant child, an innocent baby who had, moments before, been enjoying a peaceful in-utero existence, was suddenly ripped from her womb and then was thrown back into the flames to die with his mother.

That story has always haunted me.

Mia: Wow, I can see why.

Randal: Catholics were the perpetrators in that case and it would be nice if one could say "Oh, so it's *Catholics* that are the problem! Whew, that's a relief." But the fact is that Protestants have committed more than their own share of atrocities. Many of those

---

[30] Foxe's *Book of Martyrs: Select Narratives*, Oxford World Classics (Oxford University Press, 2009), 198-203.

are summarized in an Anabaptist martyrology of the era called *Martyrs Mirror.*

And even the Anabaptists, famous as they may have become for their pacifism, were not without their own stains on history. Chief among those was the debacle of the city of Munster when Anabaptists took over in 1534. They went on to butcher many Catholics and Protestants who remained in the city. Meanwhile, after God allegedly revealed a new principle of polygamy for the men of the city, wives who protested the revelation were summarily beheaded.

Mia: What?! You're kidding me! You're right, it's not just *Catholics* that are the problem. Rather, it's *Christians in general.*

Randal: No, I think it is more correct to say fallen human nature is the problem. But that ugliness certainly is present in the history of the church and it has shaken the faith of more than one seminarian.

Mia: You certainly have a flare for ferreting out the darkest and ugliest moments of your religion, I'll give you that. But I'm not thinking only of those occasional atrocities, though they are awful. I'm also thinking of average Christians, the people that might share a fence with you in suburbia. I don't know that Christians are, on the whole, worse than any other group. But I also don't see evidence that they are much better. And yet, it seems to me that this fact presents a problem. In fact, I believe that this practical reality provides an objection for many people, a reason for them to be skeptical about Christianity. And I'd like to work that into a more formal argument.

Randal: Okay. So you're suggesting that if Christians are not, on average, more virtuous than non-Christians, then that fact would constitute at least some degree of evidence against the truth of Christianity?

Mia: You could put it that way.

Randal: So then, why should we think this is true? I mean, I get that there are problems with Christians. We're definitely not as good as we should be. But how do you ground your actual argument?

Mia: The reasoning kicks off with the first premise of the following argument while the skeptical challenge comes in the second premise:

16. If Christians are being sanctified by the Spirit then Christians, on average, should display more holiness than non-Christians.
17. Christians do not, on average, display more holiness than non-Christians.
18. Therefore, Christians are not being sanctified by the Spirit.

Granted, the conclusion does not entail that Christianity is *false*, but I'd say that it comes perilously close. After all, if it follows that Christians on average are not being sanctified by the Spirit, what else does that say about the credibility of the witness of the Christian church to the Spirit and all other major Christian doctrines?

Randal: Yeah, that is worrisome. However, my first response is that (18) does not support the conclusion that Christianity is false since it is consistent with another possibility, namely that Christians have been unfaithful to our call and so may have been grafted out of God's purposes. And the New Testament carries several sober warnings of that possibility such as Romans 9:22 and 2 Corinthians 13:5.

Mia: Okay, I guess technically that possibility is open to you. But if (18) appears to be true, then that still increases the likelihood that Christianity is just false outright, correct?

Randal: Perhaps, but why should I even grant the argument? I mean, I will heartily concede that Christians are not as good as we could or should be. But it doesn't follow that we're not better, on average, than non-Christians. So how would you defend premise (17)? I get that the skeptic can readily proffer their personal anecdotes of Christians who failed to be holier than non-Christians, at least by their estimation. But that doesn't, as yet, support the conclusion that Christians *on average*, do not exhibit more holiness or virtue than non-Christians. So what is the *evidence* for that claim?

Mia: Evidence? Scientific studies may be hard to come by for obvious reasons, though presumably one could track evidence for pro-social behaviors like kindness and generosity in both populations.

However, what does our *experience* suggest? The popular Christian writer Philip Yancey once recalled asking people what they think of when they hear the words 'evangelical Christian.' He noted that folk almost never mentioned positive associations. Instead, everything they came up with was negative: angry, judgmental, hypocritical, and the like. Now that perception may not be entirely fair, but I think if you're regularly getting that kind of reception from other people, if the so-called 'sinners' are not drawn to you like they were drawn to Jesus, then that at least provides some evidence in favor of the claim that Christianity is false.

Randal: So, granting that Yancey's informal survey is reliable *evidence*, you're just going to step seamlessly from 'evangelical Christians' to Christians *generally* as if anything true of the former is true of the latter as well? That doesn't seem very fair.

Mia: I could appeal to anecdotes about other Christian groups, if you like. But what if we concede, at least, that the evidence counts against evangelical Christians exhibiting greater holiness than the general population? What would you then conclude about that group?

Randal: Even if I grant that more limited argument, would the conclusion follow? The problem, at that point, would be this: are we measuring the holiness of genuine evangelical Christians or merely *professing* evangelical Christians?

Mia: Ah, here we go: so this is the point where you say that the *real* evangelical Christians are the ones that *are* getting holier than the average person. But as for the rest of them? Pfft, you can ignore them because they're not *real* Christians.

Randal: You think it seems a little too convenient?

Mia: I think it sounds like a No True Scotsman fallacy, an informal fallacy in which a person revises the boundaries of class membership in an *ad hoc* fashion. For example, imagine that you say "No Scotsman hates the bagpipes." And I then point out, "But Doug McDougall is a Scotsman and *he* hates the bagpipes." If you then reply, "Ah, but Doug McDougall is no *true* Scotsman!" That would be the fallacy: you're arbitrarily redrawing the boundaries of what it means to be a Scotsman just to save your original claim from being falsified.

And that's what you're doing here. Every time I point out evidence that Christians are just not very good people, you reply "Oh, but that's not a *true* Christian." You're just arbitrarily redefining what you mean by 'Christian'.

Randal: I don't think so. I already noted that there are many passages in the New Testament that warn would-be disciples to examine their lives to ensure that they are, in fact, disciples. As James said, faith without works is dead (James 2:14-26). And as Jesus said in his sobering parable of the Sheep and Goats:

> "They also will answer, 'Lord, when did we see you hungry or thirsty or a stranger or needing clothes or sick or in prison, and did not help you?'

"He will reply, 'Truly I tell you, whatever you did not do for one
of the least of these, you did not do for me.'" (Matthew 25:44-45)

Those warnings don't tell us who is in and who is out, so to speak.
But they do tell us to look for spiritual fruit because that is indeed
the evidence of true disciples. And given that the production of
fruit is written into the very definition of a true disciple, you just
can't get your argument going.

Mia: I get it. So if we're only talking about *true* Christians then
they are *by definition* growing holier over time, is that it? I admit,
with sufficiently clever reasoning, you can insulate virtually any
position from refutation. But that hardly provides sufficient reason for the skeptic to find your reasoning as anything other than
pained and *ad hoc*.

Randal: In fairness, the aim of this conversation isn't for me to
provide positive arguments for my views to persuade skeptics.
It is, rather, to respond to critical objections and show that they
don't succeed.

One more thing: your objection is that Christianity doesn't seem
to make genuine Christians better over time. And to make your
case you focus on groups and averages. *But what if Christianity tends
to attract a disproportionate number of people who are at the lowest points
in their life?* In that case, the real gauge shouldn't be whether the
overall group is, on average, better than the overall non-Christian
group but rather *how has the work of God in this fellow's life made him a
better person than he would have been otherwise?* And there is no shortage
of amazing testimonial stories of that kind of transformation.

Mia: Not so fast: the problem with shifting from overall averages
to specific stories is that it frees you up to indulge in your confirmation bias by just selecting the cases that suit your beliefs and
ignoring the rest. By contrast, a sober look at group averages forces

you to consider whether those anecdotes really support the claim of objective transformation over time.

Randal: You've provided no such data yourself. And that still doesn't address my point. For example, if people on average are at a lower point of moral development when they become Christian, they could subsequently show far greater moral development over the time they are Christian relative to the general non-Christian population. But that wouldn't necessarily show up given that their initial point of moral standing was below the average. The bottom line is that we simply don't have the kind of data we would need to make an informed judgment either way.

Look, I get the emotional impact of witnessing the failure of Christians to live up to Christ. I recognize that it presents a serious obstacle for many people to consider Christianity. I just don't think it can be turned into a strong argument. It's inevitably a very limited subjective assessment. And it also misses the fact that Christians have a strong focus on original sin and the way it can impact the long journey of sanctification. In that sense, this kind of failure is precisely what one might expect in a fallen human population that is being redeemed.

21

Why isn't it unfair to damn people who are beset with significant cognitive biases?

Mia: Here's another problem I've got. It pertains to the justice of God, in particular the fact that he apparently leaves decisions about ultimate salvation and our destiny in the hands of people who are hopelessly biased.

Randal: Hopelessly biased?

Mia: Absolutely. If there is one thing we've learned from cognitive psychology, it is that human beings are indeed beset with countless cognitive biases all of which skew our grasp of reality. For example, most everybody exhibits an anchoring bias according to which we have a tendency to favor the beliefs that one starts out with irrespective of the likelihood that they are true.

We also exercise a confirmation bias, the tendency to select evidence that *favors* one's beliefs and to screen out or downplay or overlook evidence that *does not favor* one's beliefs.

Randal: Hmm, I don't see any evidence for that bias in myself. All the evidence I consider favors the fact that I critically and objectively evaluate all evidence.

Mia: Sorry, is that like a dad joke? Your lame attempt at humor is a good segue to the optimism bias, the tendency for people to view their prospects more positively than the evidence warrants.

Randal: Okay, I get it. As a bunch, we human beings are definitely biased.

Mia: Now just think what that does for our ability to evaluate our stance before God and the truth of Christianity. Consider some guy, Jones, who is raised by atheist parents who are very critical of religion. Jones is set up with a psychological profile to have an anchoring bias that favors his initial skeptical beliefs over-against the Christian beliefs that he's learned to reject. He is also wired to screen evidence in such a way that it continually confirms his skeptical beliefs and indicts the Christian beliefs he rejects. And he's wired to view his own critical reasoning faculties, his character, his entire life, more favorably than the evidence warrants, a fact that diminishes his own penchant for the self-introspection and critical awareness that would otherwise help him to discover and address his biases and sinful state before God.

While I am to believe that God wants to save everybody, yet the fact remains that God made people like Jones with a myriad of cognitive biases, biases that make it much harder for them to find salvation than it would be without those biases. Under those circumstances, to say that God wants to save everyone is rather like saying an optometrist wants his mountain climbing friends to get to the top of Mount Everest, but then he gives them all pairs of glasses with the wrong prescriptions while knowing that will make them more likely to misjudge distances and fall to their death. It just doesn't make sense.

Randal: Yeah, I agree that we are very biased as a species. And if that were the end of the story, that would be disturbing. But I also believe that God is maximally good and wise and thus he always judges people with due consideration to our limitations. When you asked about the damnation of children, I appealed to Romans 2:12 and I think it applies here as well. Paul points out that God judges Jews and gentiles differently based on the evidence available to each individual. That suggests a general principle that God always judges people with consideration of the advantages and disadvantages, the knowledge and ignorance, of each individual.

So, for example, if Smith is born suffering the effects of fetal alcohol syndrome, God will surely know that and will judge Smith differently from a person who lacked that syndrome. If Jones grows up with specific biases in light of his atheist upbringing, God will judge Jones in light of that fact as well. We don't know how God will judge people differently in light of their different starting points, but I have no doubt that he will. And thus, I have no doubt that God accommodates for our cognitive biases, at least to the extent where we hold them non-culpably.

Consider the analogy of an oval racetrack. Everybody starts the race at a different place on the track. And so, initially, Jones may be far ahead of Smith. But as the track curves around and then straightens out, eventually everyone is brought into alignment so that they all run the same distance and have the same opportunity to cross the finish line and win the race. I suggest we think in that way about how God treats us with our different starting points.

We should also keep in mind that the Holy Spirit is the critical factor in drawing anyone to faith (John 15:26; Titus 3:5) and he is not limited by our biases.

It's also important to emphasize that a person is not automatically *innocent* because they have a bias: the racist man exhibits a bias against members of another race, but he is not thereby absolved of moral culpability just because his hatreds are borne of prejudice: he will be judged appropriately for his prejudices to the extent that he is culpable for holding them.

Mia: As the story goes, the great atheist philosopher Bertrand Russell was once asked what he would say to God if he died and discovered that he was wrong. His response was to quip "Well, I would go up to Him, and I would say, 'You didn't give us enough evidence!'"[31]

Randal: Yeah, I don't see that working.

Mia: I see. So you think every atheist is sinfully rejecting belief in God?

Randal: I didn't say *that*. I actually wrote a book, *Is the Atheist My Neighbor?*,[32] in which I argue that Christians need to be careful about assuming that all disbelief is morally culpable. That's equivalent to atheists assuming that every instance of Christian belief is irrational. In each case, when you talk to specific atheists or Christians, you inevitably find that matters are significantly more complex.

But Russell's flippant attitude in that anecdote suggests little self-awareness about his own biases and little epistemic humility. Granted, he was probably playing it up for the crowd, but it is still worthwhile to keep in mind that culpable biases are built and reinforced brick by brick.

One last thing: if you were to think that I am only warning non-Christians about biases, you'd have heard me wrong. Jesus regularly warned religious insiders about their own blindspots. As we saw a moment ago, the chilling warning of the sheep and goats should keep us all checking our own biases.

---

[31] While this story has been told so often that many believe it to be apocryphal, philosopher John Searle says he was an undergraduate at the time and heard Russell give that reply at a banquet. *Mind, Language, and Society: Philosophy in the Real World* (Penguin, 1998), 37.
[32] *Is the Atheist My Neighbor? Rethinking Christian Attitudes Toward Atheism* (Cascade, 2015).

22

Wouldn't a heaven that went on forever eventually become hell?

Mia: Okay, I hope you're ready for the next question because this one might seem like it is coming out of left field. I want to ask you about heaven. Christians like you aim to get the rest of us excited about that destination. The idea, I guess, is that whatever other problems we have with Christianity, if we can get sold on this pie in the sky hope for the future, then we'll let those other problems go because oh, wow, we have heaven to look forward to!

Randal: An exceedingly cynical—and I think false—description, but keep going.

Mia: Well, I see all sorts of problems here. You claim heaven is this place of unimaginable joy that goes on forever, but it looks to me like a miserable existence. Life on a cloud strumming a harp forever? No thanks. Even if that were to appeal to you for a while, wouldn't a heaven that went on forever eventually become hell? After all, you can only sing the Hallelujah chorus so many times before you're sick to death of it. If life were to go on forever then eventually everything would get boring.

Randal: Let me start with your description of heaven as strumming a harp on a cloud. I'm not surprised that you're put off by that image: I would be as well. But that's not the Christian view. Rather, it's a mishmash of pagan mythology, pop theology, and platonic philosophy. Despite the prevalence of popular images like that, the biblical portrait of our final destiny is not about an ethereal, other-worldly heaven at all.

Mia: Then what is it?

Randal: Imagine a young man named Steve who loves art and he's always wanted to fulfill his potential as an artist by going to university and taking a degree in the field in which he can apprentice under the masters, visit the leading museums of Europe, learn how to work with clay, marble and oils.

But ever since Steve was a wee lad he has believed that when he goes to university his dad will want him to do a Bachelor's of Business Administration and take over the family auto-parts business. So every time he hears of going to university Steve thinks of having to take classes in business, economics, accounting . . . ugh. Is it any surprise that Steve cannot get excited about university?

I think that a lot of people—Christians included—have a picture of heaven that is equivalent to poor Steve's picture of university. They assume it is a destination of harps and clouds and endless singing that runs counter to all the things they love the most. And so, they have real trouble getting excited about it.

Mia: Sounds right to me!

Randal: But what if Steve has things all wrong? Imagine if one day Steve actually talked to his dad about university and his dad said "Where did you get the idea that I want you to get a business degree? Steve, I know you love art and I want you to pursue your passion. And university is the perfect place for you to do so." In that moment, Steve's view of university would be transformed from a dreaded sentence to a marvelous learning opportunity.

Mia: So the idea is that God actually has something really great in store and we're just thinking wrong?

Randal: Yes, frankly, many Christians need a paradigm shift in perspective when it comes to heaven, and I think you do as well. God isn't demanding that we set aside all the passions we have with life in this material creation so that we can leave it and go to heaven. And that's because, first of all, heaven includes God saving *creation* itself.

Mia: Er, what are you talking about?

Randal: The biblical portrait of the future is actually one of a new heaven and new earth (Isaiah 65:17, 66:22; 2 Peter 3:7; Revelation 21) which is tangible and material, a fitting home given that we'll be granted perfected tangible and material resurrection bodies (I Corinthians 15) just like Jesus. Paul describes the resurrection of Jesus as the first fruits for our resurrection: so if you want to know what we will be like, look to what he was like. The one thing to keep in mind is that the same body that was laid in the tomb on Good Friday rose again that Easter morn. Since Jesus received back his same body glorified, it follows that when we read about our new resurrection bodies we should likewise think of receiving our original bodies back renewed and glorified.

And I believe that applies to creation as well. Thus, when we read the language of new heavens and new earth, we should interpret it as referring to the original heaven and earth renewed and glorified. This appears to be the message of Colossians 1:20 which describes Jesus as saving all things, whether things in heaven or things on earth. And it is further corroborated by Paul who talks about the redemption of creation in Romans 8:19-21. So the lesson is that while we've often thought of our future home as somewhere over the horizon, in fact, we already have a foretaste of its wondrous beauty in the best moments of life on earth here and now.[33]

C.S. Lewis captured this picture in his story *The Great Divorce*. In the book people travel on a bus from a purgatorial city of grey November rain (anybody who has spent a winter in the bleaker industrial sections of the British Midlands will not have trouble conjuring up what Lewis had in mind) to the borderlands of heaven. But this world is not blurry and ethereal. On the contrary, its tangible, concrete reality simply overwhelms the senses. The colors are almost blinding. Even the grass is so real it hurts the feet merely to step on it.

I suspect Lewis is on to something here. We are material embodied beings designed to live and thrive within a material world. God has made us to find fulfillment in the very best of creation. And when we get there, it will be *more real* than anything we've experienced before, unimaginably so.

Mia: I agree that picture of heaven is less bad than the one I suggested. But less bad is not, as yet, good. I don't think you addressed my most important point, namely that even the best, most wonderful heaven imaginable would *eventually* become tedious. Here's an argument for you:

19. If anybody goes to heaven forever then they will forever live in maximal happiness.
20. Anybody who lived forever would eventually experience tedium.
21. Nobody can be maximally happy when they experience tedium.
22. Therefore, nobody can live forever in maximal happiness.
23. Therefore, nobody can live forever in heaven.

Randal: The argument may be logically valid, but why think that premise (20) is true? I see no reason to accept it at all.

---

[33] For further discussion see my book *What on Earth Do We Know About Heaven?* (Baker, 2013).

Mia: That's because you haven't really thought about what it would mean to live *forever*. You can say "Imagine how wonderful it would be to eat at the world's biggest and best buffet!" and I might agree. That would be wonderful for several years, perhaps even decades. But eventually you're going to have eaten every item on the menu a thousand times, nay ten thousand. Eventually, you'd get sick of all of it. It's just a matter of time but trust me, it will happen.

Randal: Yeah, I don't think so. There are at least two things you need to keep in mind.

First, you need to remember, as I said, that the new creation is going to be far greater than we can presently imagine. As Paul said in 1 Corinthians 2:9, "'no eye has seen, what no ear has heard, and what no human mind has conceived'—the things God has prepared for those who love him." So I would submit the issue is not that I've failed to grapple with eternity. It's that *you've* failed to grapple with the reality that eternity encompasses a range of joys and delights we cannot begin to imagine. And an omnipotent God can certainly make a buffet with ever more delectable offerings forever.

Second, I think you also need to keep in mind the joys of *re-experiencing* the same pleasures once again. Consider a mundane example. I've begun most every morning for the last several years by enjoying a cup of French Roast coffee in the cool, grey morning light. In all that time, I have not grown tired of that morning ritual. On the contrary, the rich, dark, acidic familiarity of the beverage is a particular comfort. I've had the same cup of coffee every morning for almost every one of the last couple of thousand mornings, and it isn't tedious at all. After I finish the cup I'm good caffeine-wise, at least for a while. But without fail by the next morning I am ready for another steaming beverage and I partake of the same pleasure all over again.

So why *wouldn't* that continue for a hundred thousand mornings? Why couldn't it in principle continue forever? The idea of drinking a cup of coffee every morning forever doesn't strike me as tedious at all. On the contrary, it sounds like a great way to begin every day, one of the diurnal rhythms that I truly enjoy.

Or think about the change of seasons. Where I live on the Canadian prairies, autumn arrives with a fierce pale blue sky, the yellowing of the Swedish aspens, a dusting of frost on the grass, and the honk of Canadian geese overhead. I cherish that time of year, and as with my French roast every morning, I have no reason to think I would eventually tire of the cycle of seasons (although I wouldn't mind a shorter winter!).

The same things that I say about a cup of coffee or the change of seasons are even truer in human relationships. When I value people I would always cherish spending time visiting with them and then later returning again to continue to deepen our relationship. There is always more life to share with the people you love.

Finally, at the heart of the new heavens and new earth, above all, is God himself. And there is always an unimaginable, infinite depth yet to be discovered of the God who created, sustains, and redeems all things. We cannot begin to imagine the joys that await us, as Lewis eloquently said. So I don't find your premise (20) to be plausible at all.

Mia: Maybe that's because of *your* experience. But other people haven't had your privileged experience of life. They don't have time to enjoy a cup of yuppie 'French Roast' every morning or to step back and enjoy the cycle of seasons. They're just trying to get by.

Randal: I see that you're trying to present me as some sort of out-of-touch elitist, but if anything, your comment makes my point for me. If a person finds your premise (20) persuasive, it may be because they simply lack the sublime and joyous experiences that otherwise would've helped them see how weak it really is. But I would submit that when you reflect on the best moments of a generally happy and fulfilling existence on earth now, you have a good basis to extrapolate those joyous experiences to an unimaginably greater degree into infinity, and to reject your premise (20) as a result.

I think I need to end by returning to the fundamental point that we cannot begin to imagine the pleasures God has waiting for us in eternity. Many people have quoted C.S. Lewis from his essay "The Weight of Glory" to make the point. And I'm going to join them because I absolutely think he nails it:

> We are half-hearted creatures, fooling about with drink and sex and ambition when infinite joy is offered to us, like an ignorant child who wants to go on making mud pies in a slum because he cannot imagine what is meant by the offer of a holiday by the sea.[34]

---

34 C.S. Lewis, "The Weight of Glory," in *The Weight of Glory and Other Essays* (HarperOne, 2001), 26.

23

⛵

Why can't gay people just marry?

Mia: Okay, well I say heaven will eventually get boring, and you think otherwise. Let's call that one a draw.

Randal: Nah, let's not.

Mia: But before we're done, I'd like to bring the conversation down to a far more practical question. Practically speaking, what do you suppose is the *biggest* obstacle many people have to considering Christianity?

Randal: 'Many' people? That's a vague question. Many different people could have specific obstacles that are huge for them but maybe not for others. Can you be more specific?

Mia: Too late! I'll spare you the trouble: it's your stance on gay marriage, bub. It isn't enough for you Christians that two people can simply find each other and have a beautiful life together. You need to micromanage the relationship based on some arbitrary checklist to make sure they have the right plumbing. Practically speaking, one of the biggest obstacles for many people is this one. Why can't gay people just marry?

And by the way, it seems that Christians are always behind the curve on social justice movements. Society changes and then you change after the fact. Not exactly the moral prophets that you'd like to think you are. So when are you going to catch up to the modern world on *this* issue?

Randal: I don't think your description is fair. Christians have often led the charge on positive social change throughout history: think, for example, of William Wilberforce's fight against slavery in England or Martin Luther King Jr. leading the civil rights movement in the United States. How many *atheists* have been leaders for positive social change?

Mia: Many, actually. For example, the great philosopher Jeremy Bentham was an atheist who fought alongside Wilberforce against slavery. But Bentham *also* led the charge for the rights of women and against the criminalization of homosexuality.

You know, it's also worth pointing out that there are probably twenty Christians for every atheist, so it's no wonder you end up hearing about more Christians in social justice movements because there are just more Christians, *period*. But do you hear about *twenty times* more? I don't think so. So you're not in a place to claim the moral high ground.

And anyway, in this case, the question of gay marriage, you guys are definitely way behind the times. So again, let me be very blunt: how do you justify the Christian church micromanaging the sexual lives of unchurched people?

Randal: Micromanaging?

Mia: Do you think homosexuality should be illegal?

Randal: Me? No.

Mia: And do you think that it is immoral?

Randal: I have several things to say here.

Mia: 'Several things' but no straight answer? Here we go again: the sanctified shuffle.

Randal: Yeah, or you might just let me speak without the snark.

Mia: Forgive me, but when it is a matter of human rights, I get a little testy with the endless shucking and jiving to defend the church's bigotry and intolerance.

Randal: Be that as it may, I have some important things to say and I'd appreciate it if you would extend the courtesy of allowing me to address the question in the way I see fit. If you want to criticize my view, do it *after* I've explained it, not before.

Mia: Fine, whatever.

Randal: Okay, so first of all, while this is an important discussion, it isn't at the center of Christian identity. I am a big advocate of the idea that Christians should be defined by their stance on the central topics of the Gospel: the existence of God and creation, the fall, incarnation, atonement, resurrection, second coming, and new creation.

There are many other important issues that Christians can have stances on, including ethical questions pertaining to topics like abortion, war, environmentalism, animal rights, a free-market economy, gun control, and homosexuality. But those issues should be recognized as *secondary* in import at the outset. It's not that they aren't important—they clearly are. Nonetheless, they are not *as* important for one's Christian identity as the central doctrines of the Gospel.

In recent years, I worry that the culture wars have elevated a few particular issues—especially abortion and homosexuality—from the periphery of important theological discussion to the center as if one's stance on a topic like gay marriage were equivalent in theological or creedal importance to one's stance on the incarnation and resurrection. And it just isn't.

Mia: So you're saying that Christians can disagree on the ethics of gay relationships?

Randal: The fact is that Christians *do* disagree on this issue just like they disagree on all the other issues I just mentioned. Yet, many Christians treat this question as if it were a boundary issue: if you disagree, you're not in the Christian camp. But Christians come down on different sides of that question.

Mia: Interesting, so then by that logic would you say that Christians can agree to disagree about whether *interracial marriage* is ethical? I don't think so. Surely you'd agree that people who denied the ethics of interracial marriage are straight up wrong and sinful. You'd claim their views are contrary to the Gospel. But somehow when it comes to gay marriage, you think Christians can agree to disagree?

Randal: I don't think I'm being inconsistent here at all. The Gospel, as such, simply does not include a stance on gay marriage. Nor for that matter does it include a stance on abortion or guns or any other number of ethical issues and yes, that includes interracial marriage.

Mia: *What?* Wait, so you're okay with a Baptist pastor who moonlights as a Grand Dragon for the KKK?

Randal: Whoa, no! Wow, this really went off the rails fast.

Don't get me wrong: I think it is perfectly fair to say that the Gospel lived out should *lead one* to a particular stance on any one or even all of these issues. But that's just a different claim than the claim that the Gospel itself *includes* one or more of these ethical positions.

Think about it like this. The core Gospel is that God so loved the world that he gave his Son. This should lead us to recognize human equality as Paul says in Galatians 3:28. And that recognition, in turn, can lead to a person taking a moral stance of rejecting the racism of the KKK and prohibitions on interracial marriage. But keep in mind that by the time we get to that specific issue, we've already reasoned out a couple of steps from the core Gospel claim. It doesn't mean the reasoning was illegitimate by any means. My only point is that we shouldn't make the error of now reading our second and third-tier ethical conclusions back into the original Gospel claim and thereby elevating them to a central role that they do not have.

Mia: Let me put it this way then: if you were a pastor and you discovered that your head deacon opposed interracial marriage, would you be okay with that?

Randal: Okay with it? No, certainly not. It is definitely an important issue. And I think, based on my view of Galatians 3:28—and many other passages—that it is unsustainable when the full implications of the Gospel are considered. So I understand how people can reason out to second and third tier claims from the Gospel and then conclude that fidelity to those second and third-tier implications is required *by* the Gospel. But again, my only claim is that those second and third-tier claims are not, thereby, to be included *as the Gospel.*

Hey, I can give you lots of examples of Christians who endorsed views I consider seriously wrong. For example, many of America's leading theologians of the eighteenth and nineteenth centuries—people like Jonathan Edwards and Robert Dabney—defended the institution of slavery. That is a *huge* question to mess up, and they messed up royally. But that didn't change the fact that they were still *Christian* theologians who preached the Gospel and who made some important contributions to the church.

Mia: I don't know how you justify slavery, but that seems like a rabbit trail, and perhaps you'd prefer that I go down it. I'd rather hear what you have to say about how Christians can disagree on *this* issue.

Randal: Okay, let's call the Christians who endorse the traditional prohibition of same-sex relationships the traditionalists and those who endorse the acceptance of same-sex relationships the revisionists. The first thing we should recognize is that each side has evidence to support their point of view.

For starters, the traditionalists have a consistent witness of biblical teaching to support their position including the moral prohibitions against men (*zakar*) having sex with men as recorded in Leviticus 18:22 and 20:13, teachings which are reiterated in Romans 1:24-27 and 1 Corinthians 6:9. In the 1 Corinthians passage, in particular, Paul clearly alludes to the prohibitions in Leviticus 18/20 by referring to *arsenokoitai* (i.e. man/bed) and *malakoi* (e.g. soft/effeminate men; presumably the passive role in a sexual encounter) and condemning both.

Mia: But I've heard that those prohibitions, when read in context, actually apply to pederastic relationships, like, men having sex with boys, as well as to cultic prostitution. And if that's the case then maybe the Bible never actually condemns mutual adult same-sex relationships.

Randal: That is a popular claim but I think it's wrong. There is significant evidence from the first century that people were familiar with the idea of monogamous same-sex relationships between consenting adults. This is the way that Robert Gagnon puts it, "It was well within the conceptual framework of Paul's time to distinguish between exploitative homosexual relationships and caring ones."[35] But despite that awareness, the condemnations remain unequivocal. Granted, people like Paul didn't have our understanding of *orientation* but it does seem that he was likely aware of the possibility of mutual, adult, monogamous same-sex relationships and yet he still condemned them unequivocally.

Mia: Okay, well then, *there's your answer.* If the Bible really is that clear then what's the debate about?

Randal: At this point, we need to consider that Christians do not simply derive their view of Christian doctrine and ethics solely from Scripture. Quite the opposite is the case: there are many other sources—rational intuition and logical reasoning, tradition, personal experience, moral intuition and reasoning—that also inform one's reading of the Bible and the doctrinal formulations that flow from it.

Mia: That's the idea of 'reflective equilibrium' that you referred to when you explained how the God of Abraham, Isaac, and Jacob could be the God of the Philosophers?

Randal: Yes, exactly. So, for example, consider another one of the issues on which Christians have long disagreed: whether women should be able to occupy any role of leadership open to a man. Each side has their preferred texts to support their position but the question isn't settled simply by amassing a list of biblical texts for complementarianism and another list for egalitarianism. Other factors are inevitably guiding the debate and informing which set of texts an individual is likely to accept as the primary control texts for understanding the issue.

One of the other major factors that informs the way people reason is experience. For example, if you've had an experience of

---

[35] Dan O Via and Robert A.J. Gagnon, *Homosexuality and the Bible: Two Views* (Augsburg, 2003), 81.

a woman who was a profound teacher and pastor, that is likely going to affect how you're going to read Paul's apparent prohibition of women in leadership in 1 Timothy 2:9-15. Because you've *seen* powerful women leaders you're going to be inclined to find another way to read Paul rather than as a straightforward exclusion of women from leadership positions.

Some people have no experience with same-sex relationships that are productive of the kind of social goods that we call spiritual fruit. Instead, their only experience may be salacious clips of the annual gay pride parade played back on the evening news. Consequently, that experience will inform the way they read the Bible and form their doctrinal opinions.

But others will have very different experiences. For example, I recently watched the documentary *A Secret Love* about a lesbian couple, Terry Donahue and Pat Henschel. Donahue and Henschel began dating in 1948 and remained faithful to one another for the next seventy years until Henschel passed away from Parkinson's Disease in 2019. In the film, Donahue and Henschel demonstrate the kind of fidelity, love, and mutual affection that would be considered the hallmarks of any admirable heterosexual marriage and they did so for over seven decades.

Mia: So you're saying that their relationship is as genuine as any heterosexual relationship?

Randal: No, what I'm saying is that if a person comes to Romans 1 and 1 Corinthians 6 through the prism of *that* experience rather than the prism of salacious clips of the gay pride parade on the evening news, you can bet they might be inclined to reason differently about the biblical texts in question. Experience informs the way we all do our theology and we need to become aware of that fact and recognize that this is one significant reason why Christians end up disagreeing on many topics.

Mia: That's interesting, but I think you may find yourself on a slippery slope. I mean, what if a *polyamorous* relationship shows spiritual fruit? Would you then consider *that*?

Randal: That's an important question, but don't direct it at *me* in particular. As I said, we're *all* on the slope because we are *all* influenced by our experience. The challenge for *each one of us* is to consider *when* experience has a legitimate voice in helping us formulate our opinions and when it does not. My only point here is that many revisionists consider data from apparently healthy same-sex relationships whereas traditionalists often dismiss such data *a priori* based on their reading of the biblical text.

While there is a lot more we could say about this very complicated topic, I'll just make two more points, one critical of the traditional position and one supportive of it.

To set up the critical point, I'd first like to note that traditionalists assume if biblical authors are consistent in condemning or endorsing a particular ethical action then it follows that a Christian ought to condemn or endorse that ethical action. And so, they reason that if the biblical authors condemn same-sex relationships then we can automatically conclude that we ought to as well.

However, it seems to me that matters are more complicated than that. We cannot conclude that a particular action is morally good or prudent simply because it is endorsed as such by a particular biblical author.

Mia: Based on what you said earlier about the ethics of the Torah, I guess I shouldn't be surprised that you're saying that, though I suspect it will be a shock to some Christians.

Randal: Right on both counts. The lesson is not just from the Torah, however. Another sobering example is found in William Webb's book *Corporal Punishment in the Bible*. Webb goes through all the teaching by the biblical authors on corporal punishment and he summarizes it as expressing the view that physical beatings are wise and good ways to discipline children (and slaves). Furthermore, these beatings can be inflicted with an implement like a hickory switch so as to maximize the pain; they can include lashes on the back, draw blood, be made in anger and be given for serious or minor offences.[36] That's what the biblical authors teach us about corporal punishment.

But as Webb points out, Christians today reject this teaching and we are right to do so. The reason we do so is because we recognize that this is not a wise or moral way to discipline anybody. And it's a good thing that we recognize the point, because if we did beat our children in that 'biblical' manner, we'd be rightly arrested for child abuse.

It follows that several biblical authors endorse views of discipline which are *abusive* and thus, by definition, unwise and immoral. And since we rightly reject abusive views, it follows that even consistent teaching among biblical authors is not, in itself *sufficient* to warrant condemning or endorsing a particular ethical action, at least *not if we have very good independent evidence to reconsider their opinions.* In the case of corporal punishment, I think both scientific studies on child development and punishment, as well as my own experience raising a well-mannered child without ever having found recourse to corporal punishment of any kind, all inform the way I think about this question.

As for our main topic, the revisionist could say that teaching on same-sex marriage is another case where we should question the teaching of biblical authors. At the same time, the traditionalists may counter that biblical teaching on marriage and gender relationships (Genesis 2:24, Matthew 19:5, Mark 10:8, Ephesians 5:31) is more fundamental to the Bible's message than teaching on corporal punishment and for that reason rejection of teaching on the latter does not warrant one rejecting teaching on the former.

Regardless, the debate will continue, but at least I hope you can see why I believe that reasonable Christians disagree on this ethical

---

[36] William Webb, *Corporal Punishment in the Bible: A Redemptive-Movement Hermeneutic for Troubling Texts* (InterVarsity Press, 2011), 52-3.

topic. While it is an important debate, it is nonetheless one quite distinct from the Gospel.

Mia: I get it: you're trying to be the neutral referee. So what's your final point?

Randal: My final point, as I said, is a word for the traditionalist position. First, let me preface this by saying that I don't think conversion therapy—the attempt to rewire a person's sexual orientation—is a valid therapeutic practice. That said, I *do* think God can always act to change a person's sexual orientation miraculously: the testimony of Rosaria Butterfield is an example.[37] And just as traditionalists should not be too quick to ignore the experience of gay couples in stable relationships, so revisionists should not be too quick to ignore the testimony of a former lesbian like Rosaria Butterfield.

Mia: So . . . pray the gay away? Is that the idea?

Randal: I'm not saying that kind of change is ever to be expected. I'm only saying it is a possibility and the testimony of folks like Butterfield suggests as much.

Mia: I get it, your final point is that God can make gay people straight but he usually doesn't, right?

Randal: No, that's simply the set-up. My final point, in fact, is that even if God *doesn't* do this, it doesn't follow that the traditionalist has placed an unacceptable burden on gay people. I think this point needs to be emphasized because time and again, I find gay people assuming that life-long celibacy is simply out of the question, that it is an intolerable burden which God would never place on anybody: "God wouldn't want me to be alone," they reason. "So

---

[37] Butterfield, *The Secret Thoughts of an Unlikely Convert: An English Professor's Journey into Christian Faith* (Crown and Covenant, 2012).

if I'm same-sex attracted, it follows that God must be okay with same-sex relationships."

But the truth is that the Christian life generally consists of Jesus telling his people to take up their crosses daily in acts of self-denial as they seek to follow him in holiness. So there is simply no basis to think that an unwanted call to celibacy couldn't be one aspect of a Christian's discipleship.[38]

Mia: That's easy for you to say: you are in a heterosexual marriage.

Randal: Yes, I get how that sounds. And for that reason, a person may reasonably think I lack the moral authority to make the point. But the truth of the point is independent of whether I myself have been subject to that unwanted call.

And it is also worth keeping in mind that heterosexuals regularly face similar burdens. For example, imagine a newlywed couple on their honeymoon when the wife suddenly has a stroke. In a moment their lives are forever changed: she can no longer be the mental, emotional and sexual partner that both had assumed she would be.

But *for better or for worse* doesn't have an escape clause: even if this means the husband's role is now lifelong celibate care-giver, there is no off-ramp if he is to be faithful to his vows and the call of God's kingdom in his life. Yes, it is a great cross to bear. And neither the cross of the husband nor that of the wife is one they asked for: but then, rarely do we ask for the specific crosses we are given.

While we should always be compassionate, we should also not sell short the challenge of holiness that Christianity presents to each one of us.

Mia: Wait, did you say something about being compassionate? The Christian church could definitely use more of that.

---

[38] See Wesley Hill, *Washed and Waiting: Reflections on Christian Faithfulness and Homosexuality* (Zondervan, 2016).

Randal: Yes, I agree, we definitely could. I love the example of Pope Francis in this regard. In the first year of his pontificate, he was chosen as person of the year by *The Advocate*.

Mia: Sorry, what is 'The Advocate'?

Randal: *The Advocate* is the world's most well-known public interest LGBT magazine and it has been in print since 1967. Every year the magazine chooses to honor an individual who supported the gay community and in 2013 they chose Pope Francis.

Mia: Uh, wut? I didn't know Francis was a revisionist!

Randal: That's the thing: he isn't. Pope Francis had said nothing in that first year of his pontificate to revise the church's teaching on homosexuality.

Mia: So what earned him the title of person of the year?

Randal: The cover of the magazine included the following quote from Francis: "If someone is gay and seeks the Lord with good will, who am I to judge?" His point was not to revise church teaching but instead to reorient the conversation by way of humility and an open heart. That gesture was not lost on *The Advocate*. In the accompanying article they admit that "Pope Francis is still not pro-gay by today's standard."[39] But they nonetheless selected him as person of the year because of the way he changed the church's language. The article concluded by noting "Pope Francis did not articulate a change in the church's teaching today, *but he spoke compassionately* . . . ."

Mia: Speaking with *compassion?* What a revolutionary idea!

---

[39] Lucas Grindley, "The Advocate's Person of the Year: Pope Francis," *The Advocate* (December 16, 2013), https://www.advocate.com/year-review/2013/12/16/advocates-person-year-pope-francis, emphasis added.

Randal: Um yeah, well, like St. Francis, we don't need to change what the church teaches in order to begin to speak compassionately. Mia, if there's one thing I know, it's that the church could address a multitude of our own sins if we began to speak to others with greater compassion. And that would make my job as an apologist a lot easier, too.

24

⛵

What about non-Christian religious experiences?

Mia: Okay, as our conversation winds down, I've saved a couple of my biggest, hardest questions for the end.

Randal: I can't wait.

Mia: One of the big problems with Christians is that you just focus on *your* religious experience and *your* miracles. You don't consider just how widespread religious experience and miracle claims are outside of your tradition. Pentecostals claim to speak in tongues? Well, so do Mormons. Catholics claim to be healed after praying to an icon? Well, so do Hindus. Evangelicals want to say that Jesus changed their lives? Well, Muslims will say the same thing about Allah.

I think at this point we're back to the confirmation bias. You carefully log religious experience and miracle claims that fit with *your* worldview but you screen out or dismiss everything that doesn't.

I think you need to address these questions. So what about non-Christian religions experiences?

Randal: That's a very fair question and I admit that it is a significant potential problem. Certainly people from other religious traditions do report their own experiences and we Christians need to be willing to consider how we are going to understand them. Some years ago I had a Sikh friend, an accomplished educated professional. When his grandmother died, he travelled back to India for the funeral. At the time, he hadn't been back in years. He arrived at a relative's house and was preparing to leave on the train to travel to his late grandmother's home the next day. That night, my friend had a dream in which he visited his grandmother's house and talked to her.

Mia: That's just a dream, not a religious experience.

Randal: Okay, but let me finish. In his dream, the floorplan of the house was all changed around and with notably different furnishings from what he remembered. My friend didn't think much of it when he woke up—dreams often muddle reality, right? But when he arrived at his grandmother's home, the floorplan and furnishings were *just as he had dreamed the night before*.

Mia: I admit that's weird: but weird stuff can happen. Ever heard of a coincidence?

Randal: True, weird stuff *can* happen. But his dream was very vivid and again, the new floorplan and furnishings in the dream matched the redesigned house.

Mia: Maybe he saw a photograph from a relative or perhaps someone described the changes to him. And then he subconsciously remembered that information and it shaped his dream. Simple!

Randal: I asked him about that possibility. He was emphatic that he had not seen images of the remodeled house from anyone or heard anyone mention those renovations. So I'm reluctant to say that he's just wrong about that or that it was only a coincidence. But what really threw me for a bit of a loop was specifically the fact that his grandmother—a faithful *Sikh*—had already died and he seemed to have a conversation with her in the dream just about living life and being a good person. Given that she was speaking as a deceased Sikh, the experience seemed to give the impression that he, as a Sikh, has nothing to fear in the afterlife, that his religion was just fine.

Mia: Because granny didn't warn him to repent and turn to Jesus?

Randal: Heh, basically, yeah.

Mia: If *that* leaves you unsettled, how many far more dramatic non-Christian religious experiences are there?

Randal: I don't know that it really leaves me that *unsettled*. My point is simply that other people do have other experiences set within distinct religious contexts and we shouldn't be too quick to dismiss them. And there are many, for sure.

Here's another example. Back in the years 1999-2003 I was working on my PhD in theology and one of the young scholars whose work I benefited from was a Christian philosopher named Michael Sudduth. Some years later, in March 2011, Sudduth had a nearly fatal car accident. A few months after that, on the morning of September 16, he reported having the following experience of the Hindu god Krishna which he posted some months later on Facebook:

> Upon waking I immediately had a most profound sense of Krishna's actual presence in my bedroom, a presence no less real than the presence of another living person in the room, though I was alone at the time. I responded to this felt presence, first through my thoughts that repeated Krishna's name (and inquired of his presence), and then

verbally out loud by uttering Krishna's name twice: Krishna, Krishna. I was seized at this moment with a most sweet feeling of completeness and joy. I felt as if Krishna was there with me in my room and actually heard my voice, and that my response had completed a process that began with his name within my mind. I pondered this experience for several minutes, while at the same time continuing to experience a most blissful serenity and feeling of oneness with God, not unlike I had experienced on many occasions in the past in my relationship with the Lord Jesus. It was a most profound sense of both awe and intimacy with God in the form of Lord Krishna.[40]

That unforgettable experience led Sudduth to convert to Vaishnava Vedanta Hinduism.

Now when you're raised in an evangelical conversionist tradition as I was, you are used to hearing dramatic conversion stories. And I have heard many stories like Sudduth's. The big difference is that those stories have almost always featured dramatic encounters with *Jesus*. But Sudduth's experience wasn't with Jesus, it was with *Krishna*. That right there is a big shock.

And another thing disturbs me about this case: you might think an average person could convert because—how should I put this without sounding condescending?—maybe they just didn't "know enough" about their Christian faith. But Sudduth, he was a respected academic philosopher: he knew his stuff as well as most anybody and he *still* reported that he had this transformative religious experience with Krishna. The fact that *he* converted of all people was even more unsettling.

Mia: The dream of a Sikh man with his deceased granny and a Christian philosopher converting to a form of Hinduism after an encounter with Krishna, that's not a bad sampling of strange things that should keep Christians up at night. And I particularly find that

40 Cited in "Michael Sudduth Converts to Vaishnava Vedanta!" (January 21, 2012), https://maverickphilosopher.typepad.com/maverick_philosopher/2012/01/michael-sudduth-converts-to-vaishnava-vedanta.html

off-the-wall Krishna conversion story intriguing. The dream case was somewhat ambiguous but the implications of *that* conversion story should disturb any good evangelical.

But I'm a bit puzzled, to be honest. Why don't you just play the *demon card* and say that your Sikh friend and Dr. Sudduth were both deceived by Satan's minions. You already believe Satan is a liar who wants to lead people astray, right? So what's the big surprise that he may be trying to do that here? Easy peasy!

Randal: Sure, that is easy and it is definitely a possibility. What holds me back from making that move is the Golden Rule. I would appreciate it if a non-Christian who would hear of a Christian's experience of Jesus would keep an open mind before attributing the experience to demons or delusion. So I try to extend the same courtesy. I may still ultimately appeal to malevolent spiritual agencies, but I don't *start* there.

And of course, there are lots more cases that one could consider against a Christian view. I've spent most of my professional career criticizing atheism and naturalism. I've also invested some time in considering and formulating apologetic responses to Islam and Mormonism. But the truth is that I have invested comparatively little time wrestling with major eastern religions like Buddhism and Hinduism, each of which is itself a labyrinth of distinct perspectives, arguments, and experiences. So I do wonder about some of those experiences that I've never even considered.

One specific class of cases from an Eastern perspective does stand out for me. Some years ago I read Tom Shroder's book *Old Souls: The Scientific Evidence for Past Lives* after stumbling upon it in a bookstore.[41] Shroder introduces the reader to the fascinating research of a social science scholar named Ian Stevenson who worked for decades at the University of Virginia carefully chronicling evidence for reincarnation.

---

[41] (Simon and Schuster, 2001).

Mia: Reincarnation? *Really?* And you're saying that he taught at a respected university?

Randal: Yeah, his research consisted of carefully gathering and documenting reports that look something like this: a child, perhaps four or five-years-old, begins insisting to his parents that he was killed in a farming accident in another state. He then provides snippets of detail such as describing the farmhouse in which he once lived, relaying the name and scattered details of his spouse and recalling how he died. Based on those details, the death of a man fitting that description in a nearby state is later identified and further details to which the child adamantly testified are corroborated. And what is most intriguing is that many of these cases occur in contexts, like the rural United States, where the parties involved had no prior belief in reincarnation. Stevenson documented *thousands* of cases like this.

Reading of Stevenson's work reminds me of the experience of reading another big book, *Miracles* by Craig Keener.[42] Keener's book chronicles Christian miracle claims over two-thousand years. And while the specific claims he surveys vary in their veridical force, the cumulative effect of the sweep of claims he considers is significant.

So it is with Stevenson: he wasn't some rube off the wagon. He was a psychiatrist and careful researcher in the social sciences who sought to keep an open but critical mind. And over the span of decades he amassed over *three thousand* fascinating and carefully documented case studies, some of which include young people appearing to have confident recollection of obscure events in distant regions while seeming to have no natural avenue as to how they gained this information.

In some cases, you might think there is mere coincidence at play and in other cases, perhaps chicanery. In still other cases, it may be that in some unusual way the child lighted upon some scrap of information and developed a false memory: perhaps he

---

[42] Keener, *Miracles: The Credibility of the New Testament Accounts*, 2 vols. (Baker, 2011).

or she was fed information by unwitting interviewers. All of those are possible explanations. And still, one wonders, as with Keener's work, whether there is not something more going on in at least some of the welter of cases that Stevenson documents.

Mia: Something more? Is this the point where you introduce the demons?

Randal: I see that smirk. But I'll take that as my signal to segue to a broader list of interpretive options in considering all these cases. Let me begin by reiterating that what I just said of Stevenson's work can be generally applied. In many cases, one can find perfectly natural explanations for experiences and miracle claims. And as I suggested, it is always possible that people are lying, too.

Mia: Lying? Would you say that about Christian testimonies?

Randal: As a possibility? Sure, of course: Christians can lie or embellish as surely as anybody else. So we should keep in mind the words of Jesus that we should always be innocent as doves and wise as serpents (Matthew 10:16).

However, let me return to underscore the Golden Rule. If a Christian would want other people to consider with care and charity his Christian conversion experience or his anecdotal report of a miracle, then he should likewise consider with care and charity the conversion of another person to Krishna or their anecdotal report of reincarnation. And so, whatever we end up deciding, we should always be careful not to be dismissive of the experience of others.

Mia: Hmm, okay but when are you going to get to the demons?

Randal: I can see you really want to hear more about the demonic. Yes, as I said, that is a possibility too. But let me lay out a general framework for thinking about all these cases. As I've said, it is possible that other people are lying; it is also possible that they're

deceived—and that deception could indeed be demonic in origin—
and it is possible that they're simply mistaken. Perhaps they have
false memories, maybe it is just a coincidence, and so on.

But there is one other possibility: perhaps they had an experience
that is, in some sense, genuine.

Mia: Whoa, *genuine?* What are you saying? Are you considering
becoming a religious pluralist? Maybe all religions are roads to the
top of the mountain? Christians worshipping Krishna? You're all
like blind men grapping with a bit of the elephant? Is that the idea?

Randal: No, not at all. Let me explain.

First, the Christian encountering cases outside her belief system
is, in some ways, in a parallel position to the Jew in the first century synagogue who hears these followers of Jesus the Nazarene
claiming that he has been raised from the dead. At first blush, this
sounds like a crazy claim and it didn't fit with their current beliefs.
But in a case like this, we would do well to follow the Bereans who
kept an open mind when Paul came to their synagogue and they
tested everything to see if what he said was true (Acts 17:10-12).

Mia: So you're suggesting that other religious experiences outside
Christianity could be further revelations of God just as the revelation of Jesus was to the Bereans?

Randal: No, I'm not saying that either. I'm simply noting that we
all have points where we think we have things figured out and we
are in danger at those moments of ignoring surprising new data
that doesn't fit our current paradigm. And another response is given
to us by the Bereans who simply kept an open mind and carefully
considered the evidence that didn't fit with their paradigm even
when the claims were in deep tension with their current beliefs.

I think that we should follow that example and keep an open
mind when other people make extraordinary claims. But at the same

time, as the Bereans show us, an open mind doesn't mean a *gullible* one: you still need to test everything and hold it up to the evidence.

Mia: I'm surprised, but I actually don't disagree with you.

Randal: Good, then I'll keep going. You mentioned pluralism above. So let me underscore the point: I'm no pluralist: that's the view that all religions are 'true' and no one religion has an exclusive claim to truth over the others. I emphatically reject that view as I'm a Christian and I believe Jesus Christ is God's final revelation to us. However, that doesn't mean that all experiences of God or all spiritual insights are limited to Christianity. As the old saying goes, all truth is God's truth, and at least some of that truth may well be found outside the walls of the church.

A little while ago a friend of mine recalled to me a time when he quoted L. Ron Hubbard in a sermon. Later, he was embarrassed to learn that Hubbard was the founder of Scientology. I pointed out that Hubbard can certainly say something true and there's no need to apologize for quoting a true statement. To note a fine biblical precedent, after his sojourn in Berea, Paul went on to Athens and was speaking to a Greek audience when he quoted approvingly what Stoic philosophers had to say about God (Acts 17:28). When he did this, Paul recognized that people from other religious traditions can have some degree of truth. But that didn't make Paul a pluralist. He was simply willing to acknowledge truth in whatever context it would appear. Indeed, doing so was strategic because it helped him build a bridge with the very people he wanted to win over.

The next thing to note is that God's interactions with human beings are not limited to the boundaries of the visible Christian church. Unfortunately, this is a point that we often forget. Some years ago, Bailey Smith, then the newly elected president of the Southern Baptist Convention, infamously made the claim that

God does not hear the prayers of the Jewish people.[43] As you can imagine, that claim created a firestorm of controversy . . .

Mia: Youch, and for good reason! Wow, the nerve!

Randal: I agree. Who was Bailey to say that God doesn't hear the prayers of a particular group of people?

Mia: Yes, especially when that particular group is called God's chosen people in the Bible!

Randal: Bailey seemed to be suggesting that God only tunes in to your life when you become a Christian. But the fact is that God's interactions with human beings are not limited to the church just as they were not limited to the Jewish nation before. Imagine, for example, if Abram had insisted that God could not be working in the life of Melchizedek (Genesis 14:18-20). The fact that God revealed himself in a particular way to Abram did not entail that he was not already relating in a different way to Melchizedek. The same lesson applies to Israel and the church. So we should always keep a careful dose of humility since we definitely don't have a God's eye point-of-view as to how God is working.

One more thing: our understanding of God is *always* partial and inadequate. As Paul famously said, we now see through a glass darkly (1 Corinthians 13:12). So, we should be careful about dismissing the experiences of other people simply because those experiences include faulty theological perspectives since our experiences likely do so as well.

At the end of *The Last Battle,* the final book in the Narnia series, C.S. Lewis provocatively describes a man named Emeth (Hebrew for "truth") who had worshipped a false god, Tash. But because Aslan knew Emeth's heart, Aslan states that those devout worshipful

---

43 Mark Silk, "Bailey Smith's 15 minutes of notoriety," *Religion News Service* (January 16, 2019), https://religionnews.com/2019/01/16/bailey-smiths-15-minutes-of-notoriety/

acts were in fact directed toward him: "Child, all the service thou hast done to Tash, I account as service done to me."[44] Emeth then asked whether this means that Tash and Aslan are just the same being. This question elicits a growl of rebuke from Aslan and he replies, "It is false. Not because he and I are one, but because we are opposites, I take to me the services which thou hast done to him. For I and he are of such different kinds that no service which is vile can be done to me, and none which is not vile can be done to him."[45]

Lewis' provocative scenario resonates with Paul's observation in Romans 2:12-15 that God judges each individual on the degree of revelation—or *light*—they have been given. So could God be meeting various people in various ways outside of the formal trajectory of 'official' Christian revelation? That is certainly possible.

To sum up, I offer this as a caution for anyone who is inclined to be dismissive about the diversity of ways that human beings can undergo particular spiritual experiences. We can both retain our core convictions that there is no other name under heaven by which we are saved (Acts 4:12) while also recognizing that the only one who saves may be found in places and encountered in ways that we never expected. In each case, we should keep an open but critical mind and test all things as the Bereans did. And we should always remember the chastening words of Hamlet: "There are more things in heaven and earth, Horatio, than are dreamt of in your philosophy."

Mia: Ending on a cliché? And a Shakespearean cliché no less! Nice!

---

44 *The Last Battle* (Harper Collins, 1985), 205.
45 *The Last Battle*, 205.

25

Why does God allow the most horrific evils?

Mia: Okay, I've saved perhaps the most difficult question until now, and it pertains to God's responsibility for evil.

Randal: Ahh, right, I was waiting for this topic to come up.

But before you get going let me say this: if you want a simple and effective way to identify a Christian apologist worth listening to, ask them to share their thoughts on the problem of evil. If they keep their discussion of the problem in the abstract and if they suggest that it is a matter easily solved, you should probably keep looking. But if they instead take the time to describe the agonizing depth and breadth of the problem, and if they recognize that it is such that some people reasonably find their way to non-belief, then that is likely an apologist worth heeding both on this and other matters.

Mia: So let me guess: do you fancy yourself an apologist worth heeding both on this and other matters?

Randal: I cannot tell a lie: the answer is yes, I do 'fancy' myself an apologist 'worth heeding'. Hey, I don't know everything by any stretch and I'm no doubt wrong about a lot, but I do think I have a decent approach to the problem of evil, not least because I don't try to explain it away. The minute we are ready to wrestle with the problem of evil is the minute we're ready to move from discussing evil as an abstract concept to wading into the horrific details of suffering in the concrete moments of history.

You cannot begin to offer a meaningful *solution* until you have grappled with the agonizing depth of the *problem*. And unless an apologist is willing to face the challenge on this, the most daunting of questions, you have reason to doubt that they will do so elsewhere.

Mia: Okay, I appreciate that. So then I assume you're ready to talk about the problem of evil. And by evil, I'm thinking not of bad hair days or a mild headache but specifically of the most horrible, awful things people are forced to endure: the kind of experience that rips a hole in your soul.

Randal: Yeah, I'm ready. To begin, my basic view is that God is perfectly provident over all affairs and thus he has his own morally sufficient reasons to allow all the things that occur.

But while that may make sense in the abstract, I grant that it can be nearly impossible to see the plausibility of the view when you consider it in light of concrete instances of suffering. And among the most horrendous, surely, are instances of children suffering. So to really grapple with the problem in its full horror, I suggest we camp there.

Mia: You're a brave man. Okay, let's do it.

Randal: A few years ago, I came across the case of a grieving father named Andy Whelan who posted a photo of his beloved four-year-old daughter Jessica in the midst of agony from the cancer that would soon take her life. Whelan posted the photo so that the world could appreciate the horror of childhood cancer and be motivated anew to fight it. Like countless people around the world, when I first saw this photo, I wept.

After Jessica died of neuroblastoma, this is what her father wrote on Facebook:

> I feel both sadness and relief in informing you all that Jessica finally found peace at seven o'clock this morning. No longer does she suffer, no longer does she feel the pain of the physical constraints of her body.
>
> Now my princess has grown her angel wings and has gone up to play with her friends and loved ones. She will now watch down over her little brother and ourselves until one day we are reunited again.
>
> Last night she finally allowed me to hold her in my arms and we had a big cuddle as I told her how much I loved her. I told her again that it was okay for her to close her eyes and go to sleep and I kissed her forehead and her lips numerous times. It seems like this is what she needed to finally allow her to find comfort in her passing as within eight hours of this cuddle she finally took her final breath. She was a daddy's girl from the start and even right up to the end. I feel like a massive part of me has just been torn away but I am so glad that I could give her that comfort in her final hours. She passed peacefully and calmly with not even a murmur.
>
> Thank you to everyone of you who has shared and has been a part of our journey. I ask now for privacy for us and our family as we mourn the loss of our beautiful princess.
>
> From a heartbroken daddy of the most amazing and beautiful girl.[46]

Mia: That's just so tragic.

---

[46] https://de-de.facebook.com/Afightagainstneuroblastoma/posts/i-feel-both-sadness-and-relief-in-informing-you-all-that-jessica-finally-found-p/1762089744044791/

Randal: Yes, and that photo of Jessica is but one entry in a terrible gallery of suffering children, a gallery that includes "Napalm Girl," an infamous image from the Vietnam War of a screaming, naked girl covered in that awful petrochemical jelly, as well as "The Vulture and the Little Girl," [47] a haunting image of a starving Sudanese child with a vulture lurking in the background.

Contemplating the suffering captured in those devastating images can erode our souls. In fact, while the photographer of "The Vulture and the Little Girl," Kevin Carter, won the Pulitzer Prize, four months after that career high, he committed suicide. Why? Years of covering human misery culminating in this iconic image had taken its toll: he began his suicide note by observing "The pain of life overrides the joy to the point that joy does not exist."[48]

Those are haunting words: many people have had an experience like Carter, a sense that the pain of life overrides the joy to the point that joy does not exist. In a world like that, you can't help but ask, where is God? Or even *is there a God?*

Mia: I couldn't agree more. So why don't you give up now and just become an atheist? That'd be a memorable way to end this book!

Randal: Um yeah, that's not gonna happen and for several reasons. First, in my view, one of the essential marks of these kinds of events is a deep, visceral sense that *this is not the way things should be.* It shouldn't be the case that beautiful children die of cancer, are burned with napalm, or starve to death in the desert. But if atheism is true—if we are truly in a godless universe in which we came to exist by happenstance, then there is no way things *should* be at all, there is no direction, no purpose. It all just *is* and we have to make the best of it. That just doesn't seem right to me. My deep sense of moral indignation at the wrongness of states of affairs in the world won't allow me to believe it.

---

[47] The photo is actually of a little boy but he was initially identified as a girl.
[48] Scott MacLeod, "The Life and Death of Kevin Carter," *Time* (June 24, 2001), http://content.time.com/time/magazine/article/0,9171,165071,00.html

Mia: Okay, but you've simply invited the objection back on yourself. If there is a God that, as you've said, is omnipotent, omniscient, and omnibenevolent, then why does *he* allow this great evil and suffering? In essence, you're saying that he's going against his own mandate that such things should not be. So how do you explain that? Is he like schizophrenic or something?

Randal: No, as I said, I believe God allows evil and suffering for his own morally sufficient purposes but whatever those purposes may be, the final promise is that he will ultimately wipe away every tear from every eye. In other words, the last word is hope.

Mia: Hold on: you just said that this stuff *shouldn't exist,* and that it offends your deepest sensibilities that it *does* exist. Ironically enough, at this point atheism actually fits your sensibilities better than theism because atheism isn't committed to the view that there is some overarching purpose why this suffering exists. Instead, sometimes poop happens and there is no rhyme or reason when it does.

But you do believe that there is always a reason for everything, some overriding end goal, some anticipated good explaining why God allows it. And that means that you, of all people, should actually embrace this awful suffering as part of God's meticulous and good plan. You should be *grateful* for it because you know God is doing something wonderful through it.

Randal: Look, I hate doing push-ups but I endure the unpleasantness of that exercise because of the good that comes from it. Much in life involves some degree of suffering we willingly endure for some greater good. That doesn't make the suffering, in itself, a good thing: but it can be the avenue to a good that outweighs it.

You suggested that if a person believes God does have some greater good in allowing evil that this should lead us to inaction, that I should just embrace whatever evil befalls the world because if evil occurs, God has sufficient reasons to have allowed it. But I think your reasoning is mistaken. *Our obligation, our call,* is to fight evil whenever and wherever it occurs. And we can fulfil that mandate given to us even as we know that God will ensure that to whatever degree we *fail* to prevent some evil, God will see there is a greater good to outweigh that evil which was not prevented. There is no incompatibility here. The fact is that God is always provident but that doesn't change our call to fight evil in all circumstances.

Mia: So this idea of yours that evil is always allowed for a greater good: do you think a child's dying of cancer is for the greater good of the child? Like 'push-ups' for the soul, or something? Because I find that to be really offensive. Frankly, it sounds like you're an advocate for treatments that *kill* the patient. What kind of insane logic is that?

Randal: I didn't say that. I'm not making any claim that when a specific individual suffers that the suffering should be viewed as some kind of 'treatment' for that individual. My only point is that God does have a reason for allowing specific suffering and we can be thankful for the greater purpose even as we recoil against the suffering in itself.

Mia: Well, I think of it in terms of an argument like this:

24. If God allowed a child to die from cancer then God had morally sufficient reasons for doing so.
25. God could not have morally sufficient reasons for doing so.
26. Therefore, God did not allow a child to die from cancer.

But clearly children do die of cancer. So it follows that either God is a monster, or God just doesn't exist.

Randal: Thanks, that's a good, clear summary of your reasoning.

But I would respectfully reject your second premise in favor of a very different claim and a different conclusion:

27. If God allowed a child to die from cancer then God had morally sufficient reasons for doing so.
28. God allowed a child to die from cancer.
29. Therefore, God had morally sufficient reasons for doing so.

So that's the heart of our standoff, I guess. You believe you can see God could not have a morally sufficient reason for allowing such suffering. I don't think you can see that. I don't think you're in a position to have that knowledge at all.

But that doesn't change our obligations to seek to eliminate cancer and suffering wherever possible. That is our moral mandate, even as we know that God has a reason to allow whatever suffering occurs that we fail to eliminate.

Mia: I find it profoundly offensive that you are defending the position that God has some reason to allow children to die from cancer.

Randal: At the outset, I noted that my position is that God has a reason for allowing every awful thing that happens. And I also admitted that even if people are willing to concede that in principle, the picture looks very different when they consider specific examples of suffering. So I am not surprised by the fact that you find it offensive.

But I would hope that you can tell the difference between the way we should interact with people in the midst of suffering and a theoretical discussion about the relationship between suffering and providence. If I were talking to parents who lost their child to cancer I would *never* broach the topic of apologetic responses to evil: I'd just grieve with them. But this isn't that context. We're presently attempting to have a theoretical discussion about the problem.

Mia: But you can't ignore the fact that your views have real world implications. What *reason* does God have for allowing children to die of cancer or starve to death or be doused in napalm? You say God's a loving heavenly Father. I think he looks more like an absentee landlord at best and a moral monster at worst. Why should I think otherwise?

Randal: That's not how it works. The idea isn't that I need to provide specific reasons that God plausibly has. Rather, you as the skeptic need to provide evidence that God couldn't have specific reasons.

Mia: Oh, is *that* how it works? Gee, how convenient for you!

Randal: Not convenient, just true. Think about it this way: imagine that Reggie starts the first day of a five-year apprenticeship with a master of a trade. At noon, he calls his wife and says "The master had me sweeping the floor all morning. It's a joke!" With the most sympathetic voice she can muster, Reggie's spouse replies, "Did you think that maybe he has a reason for that?"

Irritated, Reggie snaps back, "Can you *name a reason* that the master would have me sweep the floor on the first morning of a five-year apprenticeship?" At this point, his spouse would be wise not to answer. The thing is that the onus isn't on the spouse (or the master) to explain his directive to Reggie. Rather, the onus is on Reggie to argue that the master couldn't have a reason. And frankly, three hours into a five-year apprenticeship, he's not at all in a position to make that kind of informed judgment.

When I consider evil, I may not be foolhardy enough to venture into speculating on what specific reasons God has for allowing these terrible things. But I will ask, what makes you think that you're in a position to know that God couldn't have morally sufficient reasons to allow the evils that, in fact, befall his creatures?

Mia: I see, so you're playing the mystery card again. Really, is that all you got?

Randal: The issue isn't about *mystery* so much as *epistemic limitations:* in other words, we are simply not in a position to have knowledge that God doesn't have sufficient reasons to allow the evil that he does.

That said, as I suggested above, the single biggest card I'd want to play with respect to this topic is *hope.* On your view, evil and suffering happen for no reason at all: life is sometimes brutal, you suffer, you die, lights out, that's it.

But I believe in a perfectly good and merciful God, one who will indeed one day wipe away every tear from our eyes. I have hope and I cannot imagine a life of suffering without hope.

Conclusion

Why do you always play the mystery card?

Mia: Judging by the fact that you put "Conclusion" on the top of this page, I guess that means I'm not allowed to ask any more questions?

Randal: Yeah, that's the idea. In fact, you're not supposed to be around anymore. Sorry, I should have mentioned that. But the conclusion is just for me: I need to wrap this up.

Mia: Too bad, I'm going to ask another question anyway.

Randal: You can't do that. It's *my* book.

Mia: Like I said, too bad because here I go! I want to say something more about the way you just addressed the problem of evil because I think it is part of a pattern.

Randal: What 'pattern'?

Mia: Come on, you know what I'm talking about: *why do you always play the mystery card?*

Randal: That's unfair.

Mia: Don't act so surprised. You've been playing it throughout our conversation.

Randal: Hey, let's be clear that the focus of our exchange has been on problems with Christianity and my responses to them. In this conversation, I haven't focused on making a positive case for Christianity but only on responding to objections. If I show that your objection doesn't work because, for example, God might have morally sufficient reasons for allowing evil to which you cannot reliably assume you have epistemic access, that's not a copout and it certainly isn't a matter of playing a 'mystery card'. What it is doing is showing that you haven't met your burden of proof.

Mia: Fine, so let me reframe things. The philosopher Thomas Nagel once observed that "the idea of God serves as a placeholder for an explanation where something seems to demand explanation and *none is available . . . .*"[49]

Randal: I'm not impressed: Nagel is just declaring his prejudice that a particular kind of explanation, that is, an omnipotent, omniscient, omnibenevolent necessary agent cause is, by definition, not a good explanation. But I reject that claim. I think it is a perfectly legitimate explanation. In some of my other books I provide positive reasons to believe that God exists and that Christianity is

---

[49] Nagel, *The Last Word* (Oxford University Press, 1997), 132-33, emphasis added.

true.[50] And while I touched on some of those issues in this book, it certainly wasn't the central topic.

Mia: Let me try again. It has often been said that theology is like playing tennis without a net.

Randal: That's clearly false. At several points in this exchange I've appealed to exegetical principles when interpreting the Bible, as well as theological and philosophical arguments, historical traditions, personal experience, and much else.

Mia: Well yeah but, that's because you can appeal to *anything* to prop up your beliefs. It's like that parable about the invisible gardener. You know how the story goes: there were two guys walking in the woods and they came upon a clearing in the forest. The one guy says "Hey, this clearing is tended by a gardener!" and the other guy is like, "Really? Okay, let's wait and see if he shows up." So they sit. And they wait. And no gardener shows up.

But the first guy is undeterred: "Actually," he says, "it turns out that the gardener is *invisible.* Yeah, *that's it.* That's why you couldn't see him." So the second dude rolls his eyes and says, "Okay champ, what say we surround this clearing with an electric fence patrolled by bloodhounds? Then we'll see if your 'invisible gardener' turns up."

So they do that and sure enough, nothing.

But the first guy is still undeterred. "Actually," he now says, "it *also* turns out that the gardener can walk through fences. Oh, and also, he can't be smelled by bloodhounds!"

By this time, the other guy finally figures out that this dude will just keep changing his fanciful hypothesis so that it can never be

---

50 See *The Swedish Atheist, the Scuba Diver and Other Apologetic Rabbit Trails* (InterVarsity, 2012); With John Loftus, *God or Godless: One Atheist, One Christian, Twenty Controversial Questions*; With Justin Schieber, *An Atheist and a Christian Walk into a Bar* (Prometheus, 2016).

falsified. So he's like, "Dude, you just stay here with your imaginary gardener. I'm continuing on my walk."

Randal: Yeah, I'm familiar with that story. In fact, it was made famous in an essay by then-atheist philosopher Antony Flew.[51]

Mia: Whaddaya mean *then*-atheist?

Randal: What I mean is that Flew became a theist decades later. He announced his conversion in 2003.

Mia: Aw, snap! Did he visit a Billy Graham revival?

Randal: No, his change of mind was due to philosophical arguments. But that's another topic for another day. As regards this parable, I have a lot to say.

My first problem is that the story doesn't really get the way that theories work.

Mia: Wait, theism is a 'theory' now?

Randal: Yes, actually it is. A theory is an interpretive framework for putative facts, evidence, or data. Theism is one interpretation of the world and thus it is a particular theory. Atheism and naturalism are others. And the important bit is that you can always tweak a theory when evidence appears to contradict it.

I like to put it like this: theories are like cars. If you like your car, you can keep it on the road indefinitely by fixing whatever breaks on it in perpetuity. Similarly, whenever a theory needs to be revised to accommodate apparent disconfirming data, you can always revise it if you think it is worth it. That's what the invisible gardener guy is doing. But that's what *everyone* does.

I mentioned naturalism a moment ago, and that's a great example.

---

[51] Antony Flew, "Theology and Falsification," in Antony Flew and Alasdair MacIntyre, eds., *New Essays in Philosophical Theology* (SCM Press, 1955), 96-99.

Naturalism has evolved in all sorts of ways over the years. At one time, it was popular to define naturalism in terms of materialism, as the view that only material objects exist in space. That harkened back to that ancient Greek philosopher Democritus who famously said that all that exists are atoms in the void.

But gradually, this kind of reductionistic materialism was rejected because there were many non-material things that clearly existed like consciousness and mathematical objects.

So was naturalism itself rejected? No, it was revised. Naturalism then became the view that all that exists is material or arises from the material. Later, it was revised again as many self-professing naturalists said naturalism should be viewed as simply stating that all that exists is that which is described in a hypothetically complete natural science. And so it goes, naturalism keeps evolving no less than the invisible gardener.

So you see, theism is no different than any other view. They all change and adapt as theories in order to accommodate and respond to incoming data. And if you say that it is okay for naturalism to do this but not for theism, you merely show your own prejudice.

Mia: Eh, I think the real lesson is that you're good at deflecting.

Randal: And I think the real lesson is that theories change as new data comes in. And that applies equally to atheism and naturalism and humanism and other anti-Christian views. Everyone has an 'invisible gardener' in that sense.

Mia: The point of the 'Invisible Gardener' story is to illustrate that God is posited willy-nilly without any good reason. After all, in the story there is no obvious reason why an invisible gardener is suddenly invoked. The hypothesis appears arbitrary and unmoored from any evidential requirement.

Randal: Right, but as far as legitimate parallels with Christian theology go, that's just wrong. It's a strawman. Again, I've shown at least some of my reasoning here, even if it has been focused on defensive maneuvers rather than building a positive case. I don't simply invent things for no good reason. It seems to me that perhaps the single biggest obstacle to meaningful apologetic exchanges is *contempt*. When people have contempt for the views of others, they are predisposed to strawman their views and their hostility inclines them to be contrarian. Then meaningful dialogue is almost impossible. And I'm sad to say that there is no easy solution here, no straightforward way to navigate such contempt.

Mia: Well, if it's any consolation, I don't have contempt for you. It's more like pity! I just don't find most of your answers very persuasive.

Randal: In that case, the feelings are mutual! Nonetheless, I am grateful for the way you've poked and prodded me to clarify my views and address questions I might overlook. And most of all, I'm glad that you challenge me to adopt the skeptical perspective so that I can better understand the way other people see things. I do hope you'll stay around and keep forcing me to address the difficult and awkward questions.

Mia: Fear not, I ain't going anywhere. I'll continue to be that contrarian voice in your head, keeping you intellectually honest until you finally leave this mortal coil and we figure out which of us is really correct.

Afterword

⛵

Life with Your Inner Atheist

Okay, My Inner Atheist has now left the building so we can debrief. The first thing I want to say is that having this conversation was actually really helpful for me. Resolving to wrestle with several of these issues has forced me to clarify my own thoughts and confront new questions.

You may think I vindicated myself on some of the questions and that I fumbled the ball on others. But I'm okay with that because the main point of this book is not to give you a list of 'right' answers. Rather, it is to invite you into a similar conversation with your own inner atheist. You see, you can do this too. You have an inner atheist that wants to be heard. Like me, you may have ignored or downplayed that voice over the years. Or you may already be comfortable sparring partners. My simple invitation is to join in the conversation if you have not yet done so. It will help you explore your Christian faith and to consider the views of other people with a renewed rigor and sympathy. So raise the sail, catch the wind, and see where the conversation takes you.

Also from 2 Cup Press

RANDAL RAUSER

What's So Confusing About Grace?

"Smartly written and wonderfully honest."
- Eric Seibert, Professor of Old Testament, Messiah College

"Do I agree with everything Randal Rauser says and with every way he put things? I do not.
Do I think that what he says and how he says it is so sensible and so helpful that I am going to buy copies of this book to give to relatives, friends, students—even my own sons? I do."

John G. Stackhouse, Jr.
Samuel J. Mikolaski Professor of Religious Studies,
Crandall University

Buy a copy of *What's So Confusing About Grace?* **today:**
Amazon USA | Amazon Canada | Amazon UK

2 CUP
PRESS

Printed in Great Britain
by Amazon

29146781R00115